BIAS

A CBS Insider Exposes
How the Media Distort the News

Bernard Goldberg

Since 1947
REGNERY
PUBLISHING, INC.

An Eagle Publishing Company • Washington, DC

Library of Congress Cataloging-in-Publication Data

Goldberg, Bernard, 1945–
    Bias : a CBS insider exposes how the media distort the news / Bernard Goldberg.
        p. cm.
    ISBN 0-89526-190-1
        1. Journalism—Objectivity. 2. Television broadcasting of news—United States. I. Title.

PN4784.O24 G65 2001
302.23—dc21

2001048378

Published in the United States by
Regnery Publishing, Inc.
An Eagle Publishing Company
One Massachusetts Avenue, NW
Washington, DC 20001

Visit us at www.regnery.com

Distributed to the trade by
National Book Network
4720-A Boston Way
Lanham, MD 20706

Printed on acid-free paper
Manufactured in the United States of America

10 9 8 7 6 5 4 3

BOOK DESIGN BY JULIE LAPPEN
SET IN BULMER

Books are available in quantity for promotional or premium use. Write to Director of Special Sales, Regnery Publishing, Inc., One Massachusetts Avenue, NW, Washington, DC 20001, for information on discounts and terms or call (202) 216-0600.

FOR NANCY

Because she never wavered when things got dark and always understood why I had to do it . . . and mostly because my life wouldn't be nearly as much fun if she weren't in it

AND FOR BRIAN AND CATHERINE

Who bring me more joy than they know and who, without even trying, put everything into perspective for me

AND FOR MY MOTHER AND FATHER

When it comes to arrogance, power,
and lack of accountability, journalists are
probably the only people on the planet
who make lawyers look good.

Steven Brill

CONTENTS

On September 11, 2001, America's royalty, the TV news anchors, got it right. They gave us the news straight, which they don't always do. They told us what was going on without the cynicism and without the attitude. For that, they deserve our thanks and our admiration.

But it shouldn't take a national catastrophe of unparalleled magnitude to get the news without the usual biases. Before September 11, the media elites, too often, behaved badly. And they will again. It is, after all, who they are. And that is what this book is all about.

Introduction
"They Think You're a Traitor"

I have it on good authority that my liberal friends in the news media, who account for about 98 percent of *all* my friends in the news media, are planning a big party to congratulate me for writing this book. As I understand it, media stars like Dan Rather and Tom Brokaw and Peter Jennings will make speeches thanking me for actually saying what they either can't or won't. They'll thank me for saying that they really do slant the news in a leftward direction. They'll thank me for pointing out that, when criticized, they reflexively deny their bias while at the same time saying their critics are the ones who are really biased. They'll thank me for observing that in their opinion liberalism on a whole range of issues from abortion and affirmative action to the death penalty and gay rights is not really liberal at all, but merely reasonable and civilized. Finally, they'll thank me for agreeing with Roger Ailes of Fox News that the media divide Americans into two groups—moderates and right-wing nuts.

My sources also tell me that Rather, Brokaw, or Jennings—no one is sure which one yet—will publicly applaud me for alerting the networks that one reason they're all losing viewers by the truckload is that fewer and fewer Americans trust them anymore. He'll applaud, too, when I say that the media need to be more introspective, keep an open mind when critics point to specific examples of liberal bias, and systematically work to end slanted reporting.

According to the information I've been able to gather, this wonderful event will take place at a fancy New York City hotel, at eight o'clock in the evening, on a Thursday, exactly three days after Hell freezes over.

Okay, maybe that's too harsh. Maybe, in a cheap attempt to be funny, I'm maligning and stereotyping the media elites as a bunch of powerful, arrogant, thin-skinned celebrity journalists who can dish it out, which they routinely do on their newscasts, but can't take it. Except I don't think so, for reasons I will come to shortly.

First let me say that this was a very difficult book to write. Not because I had trouble uncovering the evidence that there is in fact a tendency to slant the news in a liberal way. That part was easy. Just turn on your TV set and it's there. Not every night and not in every story, but it's there too often in too many stories, mostly about the big social and cultural issues of our time.

What made doing this book so hard was that I was writing about people I have known for many years, people who are, or once were, my friends. It's not easy telling you that Dan Rather, whom I have worked with and genuinely liked for most of my adult life, really is two very different people; and while one Dan is funny and generous, the other is ruthless and unforgiving. I would have preferred to write about strangers. It would have been a lot easier.

Nor is it easy to write about other friends at CBS News, including an important executive who told me that of course the networks tilt left—

but also warned that if I ever shared that view with the outside world he would deny the conversation ever took place.

I think this is what they call a delicious irony. A news executive who can tell the truth about liberal bias in network news—*but only if he thinks he can deny ever saying it!* And these are the people who keep insisting that all they want to do is share the truth with the American people!

It wasn't easy naming names, but I have. I kept thinking of how my colleagues treat cigarette, tire, oil, and other company executives in the media glare. The news business deserves the same hard look because it is even more important.

Fortunately, I was on the inside as a news correspondent for twenty-eight years, from 1972, when I joined CBS News as a twenty-six-year-old, until I left in the summer of 2000. So I know the business, and I know what they don't want the public to see.

Many of the people I spoke to, as sources, would not let me use their names, which is understandable. They simply have too much to lose. You can talk freely about many things when you work for the big network news operations, but liberal bias is not one of them. Take it from me, the liberals in the newsroom tend to frown on such things.

And there are a few things that are not in this book—information I picked up and confirmed but left out because writing about it would cause too much damage to people, some powerful, some not, even if I didn't use any names.

But much of what I heard didn't come from Deep Throat sources in parking garages at three o'clock in the morning, but from what the big network stars said on their own newscasts and in other big public arenas, for the world to hear.

When Peter Jennings, for example, was asked about liberal bias, on *Larry King Live* on May 15, 2001, he said, "I think bias is very largely in the eye of the beholder." This might offend the two or three conservative friends I have, but I think Peter is right, except that instead of saying "*very largely*" he should have left it as "*sometimes* in the eye of the beholder." Because it's true that some people who complain about liberal bias think Al Roker the weatherman is out to get conservatives just because he forecast rain on the Fourth of July. And some people who say they want the news without bias really mean they want it without *liberal* bias. *Conservative* bias would be just fine.

Some of Dan, Tom, and Peter's critics would think it fine if a story about affirmative action began, "Affirmative action, *the program that no right-thinking American could possibly support,* was taken up by the U.S. Supreme Court today." But I wouldn't. Bias is bias.

It's important to know, too, that there isn't a well-orchestrated, vast left-wing conspiracy in America's newsrooms. The bitter truth, as we'll see, is arguably worse.

Even though I attack liberal *bias*, not liberal *values*, I will be portrayed by some of my old friends as a right-wing ideologue. Indeed, I've already faced this accusation. When I wrote an op-ed for the *Wall Street Journal* in 1996 about liberal bias among the media elites, my professional life turned upside down. I became radioactive. People I had known and worked with for years stopped talking to me. When a *New York Post* reporter asked Rather about my op-ed, Rather replied that he would not be pressured by "political activists" with a "political agenda" "inside or outside" of CBS News. The "inside" part, I think, would be me.

Sadly, Dan doesn't think that any critic who utters the words "liberal bias" can be legitimate, even if that critic worked with Dan himself for two decades. Such a critic cannot possibly be well-meaning. To Dan, such a critic is Spiro Agnew reincarnated, spouting off about those nattering nabobs of negativism. Too bad. A little introspection could go a long way.

I know that no matter how many examples I give of liberal bias, no matter how carefully I try to explain how it happens, some will dismiss my book as the product of bad blood, of a "feud" between Dan Rather and me. How do I know this? Because that is exactly how Tom Brokaw characterized it when I wrote a second *Wall Street Journal* piece about liberal bias in May 2001.

In it I said that as hard as it may be to believe, I'm convinced that Dan and Tom and Peter "don't even know what liberal bias is." "The problem," I wrote, "is that Mr. Rather and the other evening stars think that liberal bias means just one thing: going hard on Republicans and easy on Democrats. But real media bias comes not so much from what party they attack. Liberal bias is the result of how they see the world."

The very same morning the op-ed came out, Tom Brokaw was on C-SPAN promoting his new book, when Brian Lamb, the host, asked about my op-ed. Tom smiled and said he was "bemused" by the column, adding, "I know that he's [Goldberg's] had an ongoing feud with Dan; I wish he would confine it to that, frankly."

Here's a bulletin: in my entire life I have mentioned Dan Rather's name only once in a column, be it about liberal media bias or anything else. Five years earlier, when I wrote my first and only other piece about liberal bias, I did in fact talk about the "media elites," of which Dan surely is one. So counting that (and before this book), I have written exactly two times about Dan Rather and liberal bias—or, for that matter, about Dan Rather and any subject, period!

Two times! And that, to Tom Brokaw, constitutes a "feud," which strikes me as a convenient way to avoid an inconvenient subject that Tom and many of the other media stars don't especially like to talk about or, for that matter, think too deeply about.

I also suspect that, thanks to this book, I will hear my named linked to the words "disgruntled former employee" and "vindictive." While it's true I did leave CBS News when it became clear that Dan would "never" (his word) forgive me for writing about liberal bias in the news, let me state the following without any fear whatsoever that I might be wrong: *Anyone who writes a book to be vindictive is almost certainly insane and at any moment could find himself standing before a judge who, acting well within the law, might sign official papers that could result in that "vindictive" person being committed to a secure facility for people with mental defects.*

I don't know this from firsthand experience, but my guess is it would be easier to give birth to triplets than write a book, especially if you've never written one before. Staring at a blank page on a computer screen for hours and hours and hours is not the most efficient way to be vindictive. It seems to me that staring at the TV set for a couple of seconds and blowing a raspberry at the anchorman would take care of any vindictive feelings one might have.

So, does all of this lead to the inevitable conclusion that all the big-time media stars bat from the left side of the plate? Does it mean that there are no places in the media where the bent is undeniably conservative? Of course not!

Talk radio in America is overwhelmingly right of center. And there are plenty of conservative syndicated newspaper columnists. There are "magazines of opinion" like the *Weekly Standard* and *National Review*. There's Fox News on cable TV, which isn't afraid to air intelligent conservative voices. And there's even John Stossel at ABC News, who routinely challenges the conventional liberal wisdom on all sorts of big issues. But, the best I can figure, John's just about the only one, which says a lot about the *lack* of diversity inside the network newsrooms.

On February 15, 1996, two days after my op-ed on liberal bias came out in the *Wall Street Journal*, Howard Kurtz of the *Washington Post* wrote about the firestorm it was creating. "The author was not some conservative media critic, but Bernard Goldberg, the veteran CBS News correspondent. His poison-pen missive has angered longtime colleagues, from news division president Andrew Heyward and anchor Dan Rather on down."

Kurtz quoted several dumbfounded CBS News people, one of whom suggested I resign, and ended his story with something I told him, more out of sadness than anything else. Journalists, I said, "admire people on the outside who come forward with unpopular views, who want to make something better. But if you're on the inside and you raise a serious question about the news, they don't embrace you. They don't admire you. They think you're a traitor."

I am not a traitor, nor am I the enemy. And neither are the millions of Americans who agree with me. The enemy is arrogance. And I'm afraid it's on the other side of the camera.

The News Mafia 1

I **can't say the precise moment** it hit me, but I do know that it was on a Sunday night while I was watching the HBO series *The Sopranos*. That's when I started noticing that the wise guys in the mob and the news guys at the networks had the same kind of people skills.

Maybe Tony had somebody killed. Or maybe just roughed up. Or it might have been only words, something he said to his psychiatrist. I'm not sure. But the more I watched the more I saw how striking the similarities are between the Mafia and the media.

And, let the record show, I mean no disrespect to the Mafia.

In between hijacking trucks and throwing people off bridges, the wise guys are always going on about honor and loyalty and family, the holy trinity as far as guys with names like Tony Soprano and Paulie Walnuts are concerned. These are people who are exquisitely and monumentally delusional, of course. But it's this fundamental belief—that despite the bad PR, deep down where it really counts, they are just a bunch of honorable men who care about the important things in life and only hurt people who hurt them—that allows the wise guys to crush anyone who gets in their way.

It's the same with the News Mafia.

On *The Sopranos*, the biggest sin a wise guy can commit is to open his big mouth to the wrong people and blab about family business. On this matter, there is no difference—*no difference whatsoever!*—between the wise guys who operate in the dark shadows of the underworld and the news guys who supposedly operate in the bright sunlight. If a wise guy on *The Sopranos*—or one from the real-life Gambinos or Bonannos or Colombos—becomes too chatty about dirty little family secrets, there's a very good chance he will get very unhealthy very quickly.

Same with the News Mafia.

Trust me. I'm speaking from up-close-and-personal firsthand experience, from twenty-eight years on the inside as a news correspondent with one of the three big families, CBS News.

So, what happened? Well, as Tony Soprano might put it to his old pal Pussy Bompensiero in the Bada Bing! Lounge: *Bernie G opened his big mouth to the wrong people—and he got whacked!* (Which is precisely what happened to Pussy after he opened *his* big mouth to the wrong people.)

The Don in this case is actually The Dan. Dan Rather. *Capo di tutti news guys.* It's not generally known, but The Dan even speaks his own secret language, which around CBS is known as Dan-ish (it shouldn't be confused with the language they speak in Denmark). In Dan-ish, "it's all my fault" means "it's all your fault" . . . "no problem" means "big problem" . . . "don't worry, amigo" means "worry a lot, you unworthy piece of crap!" In The Dan's presence, you get the feeling that if things start going wrong for *The Dan*, something real bad could start going wrong—*for you!*

If CBS News were a prison instead of a journalistic enterprise, three-quarters of the producers and 100 percent of the vice presidents would be Dan's bitches. In the 1980s there actually was a vice president at CBS News whose unofficial title was "vice president in charge of Dan Rather." His main job was to make sure Dan was happy. This was a very important job.

But in spite of the aura of fear that surrounds The Dan, he's also one of the most generous people I've ever known. At holiday time, I would often get a nice gift from The Dan. And if you were one of his loyal guys—and for twenty-five years, I was—he'd also send nice handwritten notes telling you how much he appreciated you being around. To this day—even though he's the one who wanted me whacked—I still have an old framed picture on my wall at home in Miami of The Dan, with his arm around my young son, Brian, and me at CBS News in New York, all of us with big smiles.

And he's also funny, in a disarming, folksy kind of way. If you've ever tuned in to CBS News on Election Night, you might think you hit the wrong button on your remote and stumbled onto an old rerun of *Hee Haw*.

"Democrats and Republicans are nervous as pigs in a packing plant over these returns because the polls have closed and we don't know the results."

Must be a hot race, huh, Dan?

"Why, it's hotter than an armadillo's hide at a West Texas picnic on the Fourth of July."

How 'bout that cliffhanger down in Florida, Dan, between Dubya and Al Gore?

"That race is tighter than the rusted lug nuts on a '55 Ford."

Looks like Dubya's got the lead.

"Yeah, but that lead is shakier than cafeteria Jell-O."

Those boys sure are playin' hardball, huh, Dan?

"Nasty enough to gag a buzzard."

Who do you think will win?

"I wouldn't touch that one with an eleven-foot pole, which is the pole I reserve for things I won't touch with a ten-foot pole."

That's Dan playing Will Rogers on pork rinds. It's all written down and rehearsed, of course, but Dan makes it sound like genuine, off-the-cuff, good-ol'-boy ad-libs.

I know that Dan Rather real well. And I like him.

But a few years ago, I got to meet the other Dan Rather, the one behind the big anchorman smile. The one the public doesn't get to see. The one who operates with the cool precision of a Mafia hit man who kisses you on the cheek right before he puts a bullet through your eyeball.

So when *that* Dan assured me, sounding more like The Godfather than The Anchorman, that "Bernie, we were friends yesterday, we're friends today, and we'll be friends tomorrow"—I knew I was dead.

It was just a matter of time.

February 13, 1996, was the day I committed my unpardonable sin and began to die.

Which was what, exactly? What terrible, unforgivable crime had I perpetrated against The Dan?

Did I sell crack to his kids?

No.

Did I spill a drink on his wife's head at the CBS News Christmas party?

No.

Did I sneak into his office after work one night and make off with one of his Savile Row suits, which are tailored by the same house that made Edward R. Murrow's clothes, and which cost more than my house?

No. But I wish I had.

What I did was worse. Much worse, as far as The Dan was concerned. I violated the code of *omerta*, the sacred code of silence that both wise guys and news guys live and die by.

I said out loud what millions of TV news viewers all over America know and have been complaining about for years: that too often, Dan and Peter and Tom and a lot of their foot soldiers don't deliver the news straight, that they have a liberal bias, and that no matter how often the network stars deny it, it is true.

I would have been a lot better off if I had spilled a drink on his wife's head, sold crack to his kids, *and* stolen one of his Savile Row suits!

Actually I didn't *say* the networks were biased—I *wrote* it in one of the most important and widely read newspapers in the entire country, the *Wall Street Journal,* whose editorial page liberals love to hate. In an op-ed piece, I wrote, "There are lots of reasons fewer people are watching network news, and one of them, I'm more convinced than ever, is that our viewers simply don't trust us. And for good reason.

"The old argument that the networks and other 'media elites' have a liberal bias is so blatantly true that it's hardly worth discussing anymore. No, we don't sit around in dark corners and plan strategies on how we're going to slant the news. We don't have to. It comes naturally to most reporters."

As my old buddy Wayne, who's never set foot in a newsroom in his life, put it, "What's the big deal; *everybody* knows that's true." Maybe, Wayne, but there's a big difference between when Rush Limbaugh or Bill Buckley says it and when a CBS News correspondent says it.

This was coming from the inside, from one of Rather's guys. Limbaugh could rave on about the liberal media all he wanted and the media elites would brush him off like a flake of dandruff on a blue suit. If William F. Buckley had written, word for word, what I had written, Dan Rather would have yawned and jumped in his limousine and headed for lunch at The Four Seasons.

Limbaugh and Buckley and all those other "right-wingers"—everybody to the right of Lenin is a "right-winger," as far as the media elites are concerned—were all a bunch of Republican partisans.

But I wasn't. I was a newsman. One of *their* newsmen! I had done a thousand stories for Walter Cronkite and Dan Rather on the *CBS Evening News* and later as the senior correspondent on *48 Hours*, the prime-time show Rather fronted. They don't let you stick around for more than two decades if you've got a political ax to grind. No, I was what The Dan and his nominal bosses in the front office call all of their reporters and producers: objective . . . fair . . . balanced.

I'll bet anything those are the exact words CBS News would have used to defend me if I had reported a story for the *Evening News* that came down hard on big business or the military or even the church. CBS News would have said, *Bernie has a well-deserved reputation for being objective, fair, and balanced, and we stand by Bernie and our story.*

But this piece I had written for the *Wall Street Journal* wasn't about business or the military or the church or any other safe target. Writing about the evils of business or the military or the church is like taking a walk in the park. I had just taken a stroll through a field of land mines. Taking on the pope is one thing. Taking on the media elites is quite another. And taking them on from the inside—violating their sacred code of *omerta*—is a sin.

A mortal sin.

It's funny how some of the biggest, most dramatic changes in our lives happen almost by accident. If we hadn't gone to that particular drugstore to buy toothpaste and tissues on that particular day, we might not have met an old friend whom we hadn't seen in years, who invited us to a party where we met somebody's accountant, who walked us over to this schoolteacher whom we fell in love with and married. Go to a different drugstore and wind up with a different life.

Which brings us to Hurricane Andrew, the costliest natural disaster in the entire history of the United States, which just happened to blow through my house and thousands of others in South Florida in 1992. This brought me into contact for the very first time with a good ol' boy named Jerry Kelley, a chain-smoking, fifty-something building contractor who grew up in Enterprise, Alabama, and who makes Gomer Pyle sound like Laurence Olivier.

Without Hurricane Andrew there would have been no Jerry Kelley. And without Jerry Kelley there would have been no *Wall Street Journal* op-ed piece that changed my life forever.

Jerry Kelley saved my family and me. He repaired the damage the hurricane had done to our house. He was always there when we needed him. And we became friends, a kind of odd couple. We talked often, mostly about politics and current events, which he loved.

And on February 8, 1996, Jerry Kelley called me at home, wondering whether I had caught the *CBS Evening News* that night.

"Did you see that 'Reality Check' story on Dan Rather tonight?" he wanted to know, sounding even more like a cracker than he usually did, if that was possible. Jerry wasn't an angry kind of guy, but he was pretty hot that night. I told him I missed the Dan Rather newscast and asked what the problem was.

"The problem," he said, "is that you got too many snippy wise guys doin' the news, that's what the problem is." We went around like this for a while, and he told me to get a tape of the news and watch it. Then "you tell me if there's a problem."

Fair enough. The next day I went into the CBS News bureau in Miami to watch a videotape of the story that had Jerry so worked up.

The reporter was Eric Engberg, a Washington correspondent whose "Reality Check" was about presidential candidate Steve Forbes and his flat tax, which was the centerpiece of the Forbes campaign.

Not exactly a sexy subject. So what's the big deal, I wondered. But as I watched the videotape, it became obvious that this was a hatchet job, an editorial masquerading as real news, a cheap shot designed to make fun of Forbes—a rich conservative white guy, the safest of all media targets—and ridicule his tax plan.

Still, blasting the flat tax wasn't in the same league as taking shots at people who are against affirmative action or abortion, two of the more popular targets of the liberal media elites. How worked up was I supposed to get . . . *over the flat tax?*

But the more I watched the more I saw that this story wasn't simply about a presidential candidate and a tax plan. It was about something much bigger, something too much of big-time TV journalism had become: a showcase for smart-ass reporters with attitudes, reporters who don't even pretend to hide their disdain for certain people and certain ideas that they and their sophisticated friends don't particularly like.

Rather introduced Engberg's piece with the standard stuff about how it would "look beyond the promises to the substance" of the

Forbes flat tax. Television news anchors enjoy using words like "substance," mostly because a half-hour newscast (about twenty-one minutes after commercials) has so little of it.

Engberg's voice covered pictures of Steve Forbes on the campaign trail. "Steve Forbes pitches his flat-tax scheme as an economic elixir, good for everything that ails us."

Scheme? Elixir? What the hell kind of language is that, I wondered? These were words that conjured up images of con artists, like Doctor Feelgood selling worthless junk out of the back of his wagon.

But that was just a little tease to get us into the tent. Then Engberg interviewed three different tax experts. Every single one of them opposed the flat tax. Every single one! Where was the fairness and balance Rather was always preaching about? Wasn't there any expert—*even one*—in the entire United States who thought the flat tax *might* work?

Of course there was. There were Milton Friedman and Merton Miller, both of the University of Chicago and both Nobel Prize winners in economics. There was James Buchanan of George Mason University, another Nobel laureate. There were also Harvey Rosen of Princeton, William Poole of Brown, and Robert Barro of Harvard. All of them were on the record as supporting the flat tax to one degree or another.

Engberg could have found a bunch of economists to support the flat tax, *if he had wanted to.* But putting on a supporter of the flat tax would have defeated the whole purpose of the piece, which was to have a few laughs at Steve Forbes's expense.

There is absolutely no way—not one chance in a million—that Engberg or Rather would have aired a flat-tax story with that same contemptuous tone if Teddy Kennedy or Hillary Clinton had come up with the idea.

But even if you opposed the flat tax, even if you thought it was a bad idea that helped only the wealthiest Americans—fat cats like Steve Forbes himself—what about simple journalistic fairness? What about presenting two sides? Isn't that what Rather was always saying CBS News was about: objectivity, fairness, balance?

And then Engberg crossed that fuzzy little line that's supposed to separate news from entertainment. He decided it was time to amuse his audience. And who could blame him? The flat tax didn't have much pizzazz by showbiz standards. The audience might lose interest and, God forbid, change the channel. In the United States of Entertainment there is no greater sin than to bore the audience. A TV reporter could get it wrong from time to time. He could be snippy and snooty. But he could not be boring.

Which is why Eric Engberg decided to play David Letterman and do a takeoff of his Top Ten list.

"Forbes's Number One Wackiest Flat-Tax Promise," Engberg told the audience, is the candidate's belief that it would give parents "more time to spend with their children and each other."

Wacky? This was a perfectly acceptable word in the United States of Entertainment to describe, say, a Three Stooges movie. Or *Hamlet*, starring Jerry Lewis. Or *My Fair Lady*, with Chris Rock playing Professor Higgins.

But "wacky" seemed an odd word to describe a serious idea to overhaul America's ten-trillion-page tax code that enables lobbyists to donate tons of money to politicians who then use this same Byzantine tax code to hand out goodies to the very same special interests that just gave them all that money. If anything is "wacky," it's the *current* tax system, not an honest attempt to replace it with something new.

Besides, what Forbes meant is that since many Americans—not just the wealthy—would pay less tax under his plan, they might not have to work as many hours and might actually have more time to spend at home with their families. Maybe it's true and maybe it isn't, but is "wacky" the fairest and most objective way to describe it?

Can you imagine, in your wildest dreams, a network news reporter calling Hillary Clinton's health care plan "wacky"? Can you imagine Dan Rather or any other major American news anchorman allowing it?

And finally, the coup de grâce, the knife to Steve Forbes's throat as Engberg went on camera to end his story. The "on camera," as we call it in the TV news business, is when the reporter gets to look the viewer in the eye and deliver a sermonette. This is when the reporter, if he hasn't been slanting the news up to this point, will often give you a little editorial just to make sure you know how you're supposed to think about the subject at hand. Eric Engberg ended his little vaudeville act thus: "The fact remains: The flat tax is a giant, untested theory. One economist suggested, before we put it in, we should test it out someplace—like Albania." Engberg flashed his signature smirk and signed off—"Eric Engberg, CBS News, Washington."

There is junk science, junk food, and junk bonds. This was junk journalism.

I don't believe for a second that Eric Engberg woke up that morning and said, "I think I'll go on the air tonight and make fun of Steve Forbes." The problem is that so many TV journalists simply don't know what to think about certain issues until the *New York Times* and the *Washington Post* tell them what to think. Those big, important newspapers set the agenda that network news people follow. In this case the message from Olympus was clear: We don't like the flat tax. So neither did Eric Engberg, and neither did anyone at CBS News who put his story on the air. It's as simple as that.

That the flat tax was a conservative idea only made the job of bashing it more fun. Yes, it's true that a number of conservative politicians came out against it. Lamar Alexander, for one, called it "a truly nutty idea." But Alexander, and some others who came out against Forbes's version of the flat tax—like Pat Buchanan, who said it was a plan that favored "the boys down at the yacht basin"—just happened to be running for president against Steve Forbes. That raises a few legitimate questions about their motives.

Make no mistake: the flat tax *is* fundamentally conservative. In *Newsweek*, George Will wrote, "In the 1990s conservatism had two genuinely radical proposals for domestic reform, proposals that would have fundamentally altered the political culture. Term limits for members of Congress would have ended careerism, today's strongest motive for entering, and for particular behavior in, politics. A flat tax would have taken the tax code out of play as an instrument for dispensing political favors, and would have put out of business a parasite class of tax lawyers and lobbyists in Washington."

By and large, the angst over the flat tax came from the Left. Which makes perfect sense. Liberals have an uneasy feeling about tax cuts in general and are downright hostile to the kinds of cuts that benefit the wealthy in particular, even if they also help a lot of other Americans. They may argue against the flat tax on economic grounds, which is fair enough since there are legitimate questions and concerns about a flat-tax rate. But much of the opposition from the Left had little to do with economics. It was visceral, from the same dark region that produces envy and the seemingly unquenchable liberal need to wage class warfare.

Paul Begala, the political strategist who worked on both the 1992 and 1996 Clinton-Gore campaigns, charmingly explained the Left's philosophy on people with money when, according to Bob Woodward's *The Agenda*, he told Treasury Secretary Robert Rubin, "Fuck them [the rich]."

Karl Marx couldn't have said it better.

So the Left routinely uses words like "scheme" instead of the more neutral "plan" to describe tax cuts that favor "the wrong people." Sometimes they put the word "risky" before "scheme" to make it sound really scary. Al Gore did precisely that, about a hundred times a day, when he was running for president against George W. Bush. I understand why Al Gore and other liberals call something they don't like a "scheme." Politicians and partisans are allowed to do that. But should supposedly objective people like news reporters, people like Eric Engberg, use that kind of loaded language? Should a journalistic enterprise like CBS News—which claims to stand for fairness and objectivity—allow words like "scheme" and "wacky" in what is supposed to be a straight news story about a legitimate candidate running for president of the United States?

Engberg's piece—its strident, mocking tone, its lack of objectivity, its purposeful omission of anyone who supported the flat tax—was like a TV campaign commercial paid for by *Opponents of the Steve Forbes Flat Tax*.

From top to bottom the Engberg piece was breathtaking in its lack of fairness. So how could CBS put it on the air? Well, news fans, here's one of those dirty little secrets journalists are never supposed to reveal to the regular folks out there in the audience: a reporter can find an expert to say anything the reporter wants—*anything!* Just keep calling until one of the experts says what you need him to say and tell him you'll be right down with your camera crew to interview him. If you find an expert who says, "You know, I think that flat tax just might work and here's why..." you thank him, hang up, and find another expert. It's how journalists sneak their own personal views into stories in the guise of objective news reporting. Because the reporter can always say, "Hey, I didn't say the flat tax stinks—the guy from that Washington think tank did!"

It happens all the time.

I don't know Steve Forbes. I've never met him. I don't even buy his magazine. *And I had never voted for a Republican candidate for president in my entire life!* But he was a serious, intelligent man seeking the most important job in our country, and what CBS News had just done to him was shameful and not worthy of an important network news organization.

So I called Jeff Fager, who had just taken over as executive producer of the *CBS Evening News*. I had known Jeff for more than ten years. I asked him how in the world he could have put that story on the air. Fager didn't remember any details of the Engberg report. That's how *un*controversial it was to him.

I told Fager I had been complaining privately about bias at CBS News for years, that I always kept it in-house, but this time was different. This time, I told him, I was going to write about it, and then maybe he and the other people who decide what gets on the air would listen.

Jeff Fager is an interesting guy. Funny. Smart. Easygoing. But in some ways he's *too* cool. Nothing fazes him. Jeff is the kind of guy who never suffers a crisis of confidence, not on the outside where you could tell, anyway. From what I could tell by working with him over the years, Jeff is someone who is more in touch with his "inner self" than all those self-esteem gurus who show up on PBS during a pledge drive *put together*. Which is probably why he wasn't upset with the Engberg hatchet job. So I sat down and started writing the op-ed piece.

The way I saw it, I wasn't taking on Engberg or Rather or CBS News for airing one snooty story about some politician's tax plan. For me, this was about a nagging problem that none of the big shots would take seriously. It was about the liberal biases that overwhelm straight news reporting.

I knew, of course, that The Dan didn't tolerate dissent.

I knew that to Dan Rather dissent was betrayal. As Andrew Heyward, the president of CBS News, once told me: "Dan can't distinguish between mainstream, legitimate criticism and criticism coming from extremists. It's all the same to him. He just can't separate one from the other." Heyward also said, "If anyone around here ever takes Dan on, he'll find a way to get even."

Even though I knew how unforgiving Dan might be, I sure as hell wasn't trying to be a martyr. I couldn't afford to lose my job over this, not with a mortgage, wife, and kids. My son, Brian, by this time was at Carnegie Mellon University, where the cost of tuition is about the same as the cost of the space shuttle. My daughter, Catherine, who was only seven, would be in college soon enough.

CBS News was paying the bills, and I wasn't about to throw it all away because of a lousy piece on the evening news. But I felt I had to say something where it might get attention and have some impact. My in-house protests hadn't worked, but maybe an op-ed in the *Wall Street Journal* would open my colleagues' eyes to what everyone else could see—the bias that showed up too often on the evening news.

Over the years I had spoken to Heyward and a few others dozens of times about bias on the evening news and other programs. You can't talk directly to the anchorman about such things, because anchormen in general don't do well with criticism. They're like royalty. Which means everyone is always kissing their royal ass, and after a while they behave more like kings than journalists. Sure, they may have to take crap from time to time from those pain-in-the-ass TV critics, but guys like Dan Rather sure as hell aren't about to take it from their own reporters, no matter how diplomatically we might deliver it. And if you offend The Dan, The Dan can keep you off the air, which for a TV reporter can be a very bad thing—like the end of your livelihood.

The bias I'm talking about, by the way, isn't so much political bias of the Democratic-versus-Republican sort. There is that, for sure, but I know that reporters would tear down their own liberal grandmothers if they thought it would make them look tough and further their careers. For me that isn't the real problem. The problem comes in the big social and cultural issues, where we often sound more like flacks for liberal causes than objective journalists.

Why were we doing the work of the homeless lobby by exaggerating the number of homeless people on the streets of America? And why were we portraying them as regular folks just like you and me when we all knew they were overwhelmingly alcoholics and drug addicts and schizophrenics?

Why were we doing PR for the AIDS lobby by spreading an epidemic of fear, telling our viewers about how AIDS was about to break out into mainstream heterosexual America, which simply was not true?

Why did we give so much time on the evening news to liberal feminist organizations, like NOW, and almost no time to conservative women who oppose abortion?

I always had expressed my concerns privately, like a good, if somewhat disgruntled, soldier. All I wanted was a discussion, someone to take these concerns seriously. But no one ever did.

I admit it: when I got off the phone with Jeff Fager, I was angry. Maybe it was what I perceived as his indifference. To this day I'm not sure. I just felt that I had to make my case.

Out loud.

Jerry Kelley from Enterprise, Alabama, spotted the bias in the Engberg report. Jerry Kelley spotted the wise guy tone and the one-sidedness. And Jerry Kelley is a general building contractor, not a newsman.

Who didn't find anything wrong with Engberg's piece?

First off, Engberg didn't.

His producer in Washington didn't.

The *Evening News* senior producer in Washington didn't.

Jeff Fager, the executive producer of the *CBS Evening News* in New York, didn't.

His team of senior producers in New York didn't.

Andrew Heyward, the CBS News president and Harvard Phi Beta Kappa, didn't.

And finally, Dan Rather, the anchorman and managing editor of the *CBS Evening News*, didn't.

Not one of them spotted anything wrong with a story that no one should have let on the air in the first place.

These are people so sensitive and so "in tune" with our politically correct times that they'd practically go into cardiac arrest if a reporter used the word "Indian" instead of "Native American" on the air. Or said "handicapped" instead of "disabled"—or better yet, "physically challenged." These journalists can spot a slight a mile away but could not see anything wrong with one of their own mocking the flat tax proposed by a rich white guy running for the Republican presidential nomination.

So how was Jerry Kelley able to see something that all the high-priced, big-shot network journalists couldn't see? It's easy. Jerry's not part of their crowd. More to the point, they'd rather eat rat poison than be part of his.

Except for Rather. Rather might wear custom-tailored British suits and live on Park Avenue, but he has never forgotten his own roots: that his father, "Rags," dug ditches in East Texas during the Great Depression while his mother, Byrl, was a waitress. Most of the others don't know people like Jerry Kelley, or people like Dan's father or mother, for that matter. They don't have blue-collar people like that in their families. They don't have blue-collar friends, and they don't want any. They don't talk to people like Jerry Kelley, and they certainly don't listen to people like Jerry Kelley.

Too many news people, especially the ones at worldwide headquarters in New York, where all the big decisions are made, basically talk to other people just like themselves. What the journalist John Podhoretz said about New Yorkers in general is especially true of the New York media elite in particular: they "can easily go through life never meeting anybody who has a thought different from their own."

Far-fetched? Just think back to that famous observation by the *New Yorker*'s otherwise brilliant film critic Pauline Kael, who in 1972 couldn't figure out how Richard Nixon had won the presidency.

"I can't believe it!" she said. "I don't know a single person who voted for him!" *Nixon carried forty-nine states to McGovern's one, for God's sake—and she wasn't kidding!*

That's one of the biggest problems in big-time journalism: its elites are hopelessly out of touch with everyday Americans. Their friends are liberals, just as they are. They share the same values. Almost all of them think the same way on the big social issues of our time: abortion, gun control, feminism, gay rights, the environment, school prayer. After a while they start to believe that all civilized people think the same way they and their friends do. That's why they don't simply disagree with conservatives. They see them as morally deficient.

What *reasonable* person, they wonder, could possibly be *against* affirmative action? Maybe some stupid people in the South and Midwest who wear polyester pants are against it. But what could you expect from *them*, anyway?

The sophisticated media elites don't categorize their beliefs as liberal but as simply *the correct way to look at things*. They think they're middle of the road—raging moderates—while everyone else (the people who live in the "red states" that George W. Bush carried) is on the fringe. It's scary to think that so many important people who bring Americans the news can be so delusional.

David Awbrey, once the editorial page editor of the *Wichita Eagle* in middle-America Kansas, had it right: "With their six-figure salaries, establishment journalists have little understanding of how hard it is to raise a family on a working-class paycheck. They are more likely to vacation in London or on Martha's Vineyard than in Branson or at Disney World. And from their gilded Manhattan and Georgetown ghettoes, many of them look contemptuously upon such towns as Wichita, Omaha, and Des Moines as little more than overgrown gopher prairies as depicted in Sinclair Lewis's *Main Street*."

So I wrote the op-ed piece. In it I said, "It's not just Democrats and some Republican presidential candidates who don't like the flat tax—it's also a lot of big-time reporters. The flat tax rubs them the wrong way. Which is fair enough—until their bias makes its way into their reporting."

I wrote about the liberal bias that permeates the national press, and I dissected Engberg's "Reality Check" point by point, showing how slanted it was. Then I wrote, "One thing to remember about network news is that it steals just about everything from print. So if the *New York Times* is against the flat tax, and the *Washington Post* is against the flat tax, the networks can't and won't be far behind."

I concluded with this: "'Reality Check' suggests the viewers are going to get the facts. And then they can make up their mind. As Mr. Engberg might put it: 'Time out!' You'd have a better chance of getting the facts someplace else—like Albania."

A few hours after I faxed the op-ed to the *Wall Street Journal*, I got a call back from an editor named David Asman (now with the Fox News Channel). He told me he liked the piece and that "We're going to run it next Tuesday."

"Be prepared," I sighed, "to run my obituary next Wednesday."

Mugged by "The Dan" **2**

It wasn't a phone call I was anxious to make, but I knew I had to. The Dan was in Iowa on February 12, 1996, covering the presidential caucuses. I was at the CBS Broadcast Center in New York. I wanted to give him a heads-up, an early warning about the *Wall Street Journal* piece that would be coming out the next morning.

"I wrote a piece for the *Wall Street Journal*, Dan, and my guess is you won't be ecstatic about it."

I hadn't given him any particulars yet, so before I could go on, he assured me that it couldn't be that bad. "Bernie," he told me, "we were friends yesterday, we're friends today, and we'll be friends tomorrow."

"So tell me about it," he said, sounding mildly curious but not especially concerned. I told him it was about a story that had run on his evening newscast a few days earlier. That it was about how the story was cynical and biased and loaded with cheap shots aimed at one of the candidates running for president. I also told him about how the supposedly objective news story was part of an ongoing problem at the networks.

When I finished with my early warning, my friend the anchorman, who wasn't going to let some *Wall Street Journal* piece stand in the way of our friendship, told me, "I'm getting viscerally angry about this."

Angry, I was expecting. What came next, I wasn't.

Rather's voice started quavering, and he told me how in his younger days he had signed up with the marines—not once, but twice!

What the hell did that have to do with anything?

He emphasized that this happened during "peacetime"—to his credit, he was trying not to sound like some kind of war hero. Rather was famous for coming close to tears *on the air* when he had a patriotic story about Memorial Day or the Vietnam Wall or something like that. Now he was doing it with me, over the phone.

Where was he going with this? I was telling him the media elites have a liberal bias, and he was telling me he was a marine who loved his country!

And then it hit me: somehow, Dan Rather, red, white, and blue American, Texan, ex-marine-and-damn-proud-of-it, thought that if I believed the *CBS Evening News* (and the ABC and NBC news programs, too) tilted left then I must be suggesting that it's just a short hop from being a liberal to being . . . *an unpatriotic American!* Sure it's crazy, but why else would he tell me that he signed up with the marines, twice?

I also spoke to Heyward and Engberg, dropping an advance copy at Heyward's office. When Heyward called me it was obvious that steam was coming out of his ears. What I had done, he told me, was "an act of disloyalty" and "a betrayal of trust."

"I understand how you feel," I told him, trying to defuse a bad situation. "But I didn't say anything in the piece about how even you, Andrew, have agreed with me about the liberal bias."

Instead of calming things down, my comment made him go ballistic.

"That would have been like raping my wife and kidnapping my kids!" he screamed at me. If there was an instant when I knew just how dark

things would get, this was it. This one, frantic statement—*That would have been like raping my wife and kidnapping my kids*—told me everything I needed to know about the magnitude of my sin.

Writing an op-ed piece was like *raping his wife and kidnapping his kids.* Criticizing, publicly, what I saw as bias in network news was like *raping his wife and kidnapping his kids.*

This is how self-centered the media elites can be. These are people who routinely stick their noses into everybody else's business. These are people who are always telling us about the media's constitutional right to investigate and scrutinize and a lot of times even embarrass anyone who winds up in our crosshairs. These are people who love to take on politicians and businessmen and lawyers and Christians and the military and athletes and all sorts of other Americans, yet when one of their own writes an opinion piece about *American Journalism*, then you've crossed the line . . . because taking on the media is like *raping their wives and kidnapping their kids!*

Engberg was just as angry—but not nearly as enchanting. I called him at the CBS News Washington bureau and told him what the op-ed was about. I said it was an issue that needed to be discussed, and that since no one would listen in-house, I felt I had to go public. I told him "my intent is not to hurt you or anyone else."

Engberg listened without saying a word. When I finished he said, "Okay, Bernie, here's my response: You're full of shit." Then he hung up and has never spoken to me again.

Dan Rather, the man who assured me "we were friends yesterday, we're friends today, and we'll be friends tomorrow," hasn't spoken a word to me, either. I could have taken out a full-page ad in the *New York Times* saying Dan Rather wears black stiletto do-me heels and red miniskirts behind the anchor desk, and he wouldn't have gotten as mad as when I said we have a bias problem in the media. Dan Rather, the ex-marine, felt as if he had just been shot . . . *by one of his own troops.*

In a flash, I had become Richard Nixon and Spiro Agnew and every other "right-wing, ideological nut" who at one time or another tried to take Dan Rather down.

Right after the *WSJ* piece came out, I was taken off the air, pending some decision on whether I would be fired. I sent Dan two letters, which I made sure were hand-delivered, explaining why I did what I did and telling him my intent wasn't to hurt him personally but to finally get a conversation going about this bias problem.

He ignored both.

Many of my colleagues, the news liberals who had always preached openness and tolerance, stopped talking to me, fearing my radioactivity would rub off on them. But then, in the elegant phrase of the journalist Brian Brown, liberals these days have forgotten how to be liberal. After a quarter of a century at CBS News—half my entire life!—I had become a nonperson.

The day the op-ed piece came out I got a phone call from Asa Baber, a close friend who writes the "Men" column in *Playboy*. "I just read your *Wall Street Journal* piece," he said, "and I would suggest you call the FBI and see if they'll put you in the Witness Protection Program."

If I had had the number handy, I would have.

CBS News has always liked to think of itself as a family. But from where I was standing—isolated, off the air, and under fire as part of the vast right-wing conspiracy—it was looking more and more like the Manson Family.

When Michelle Greppi of the *New York Post* interviewed Rather and asked about my op-ed piece, he told her, "The test is not the names people call you or accusations by political activists inside or outside your own organization."

Political activist? Time to take a taxi back to Earth, Dan.

Here's what I would have asked The Dan if I had had the opportunity, which I did not, since he wasn't talking to me:

1. When did I sell out and become this "political activist"?
2. What have I *ever* done to deserve that description?
3. How long had you known about my "political activism"?
4. How is it that you never called me a "political activist" *before* I wrote the op-ed piece?
5. Could it be that I became a "political activist" at precisely the moment I pointed out this liberal bias that only you and a few others still deny exists?

This was the strategy The Dan had settled on. Protect your own image by ripping your accuser. If Dan could discredit me and divert attention from what I wrote about the media elites, if he could focus attention instead on my newly discovered right-wing ideology, then—who knows?—maybe he could convince people that there really is no liberal bias in the news and that I really am a political activist, maybe even on the payroll of Jesse Helms. Anything is possible.

Isn't this exactly what politicians do all the time—often with great success—when they get caught doing something they shouldn't be doing? They attack their accusers. If politicians could get away with it, why not big-time television news stars?

In the same *New York Post* interview Greppi told Rather, "Peter Jennings has said, to the chagrin of some people at ABC News, that he thinks the conservative voice is sometimes not heard in network news. Bernard Goldberg said much the same recently in the *Wall Street Journal*."

Rather came back with one of those off-the-wall and over-the-top salvos that sound kind of funny until you realize he's not joking.

"I will put up billboard space on 42nd Street. I will wear a sandwich board. I will do whatever is necessary to say I am not going to be cowed by anybody's special political agenda, inside, outside, upside, downside."

So I wasn't simply a "political activist" as far as The Dan was concerned. I was a "political activist" *with* a "political agenda." How in the world had I survived twenty-five years at CBS News, much of that time working for Dan Rather himself, if I was a political activist with a political agenda?

What made Dan's rant even more transparent was that just four months earlier, when I returned to the *CBS Evening News* after seven years away in prime time, on *48 Hours* and *Eye to Eye* with Connie Chung, Rather looked into the camera and told millions of people in his audience, "Tonight on the *CBS Evening News* we're pleased to welcome back to our broadcast veteran correspondent, colleague, and friend Bernard Goldberg to share his unique perspectives on events of the day."

How was it that I was such a pro in October of 1995 when Dan welcomed me back to the evening news and such a bum in February of 1996 when my *WSJ* piece came out? How did I go from being a featured reporter on the *CBS Evening News* with my own special segment—"Bernard Goldberg's America"—to such a right-wing scoundrel, virtually overnight?

When Ed Bark of the *Dallas Morning News* interviewed him about my column, Rather said, "If you want to see my neck swell and the hair on the back of my neck rise, you just try to tell me how to report the news. When anybody tries to intimidate me into reporting the news their way, my answer is, 'Get lost.' I've never done it. I'm not going to do it now."

Was this genuine paranoia, I wondered, or just part of the act? Now I was trying to "intimidate" him into covering the news my way. Why is it that when journalists write something tough about *other* people, it's called "news," but when someone writes something tough about *news people* like Dan Rather, it's called "intimidation"?

They love diversity in the newsroom. That's what they say, anyway. They love diversity of color, diversity of gender, diversity of sexual orientation. But God forbid someone in their diverse newsroom has a diverse view about how the news ought to be presented. When that happens, these champions of diversity quake in their boots and practically make in their pants.

In fact, Andrew Heyward, the president of the news division, told the *Washington Post* that my op-ed column had caused "a great deal of residual pain and suffering." *Pain and suffering?* Reporters who see more death and destruction than the Red Cross were in *pain and suffering* over . . . *my opinion?*

Reporters who cover plane crashes and tornadoes, and who see dead bodies being pulled from debris, these tough reporters were experiencing *pain and suffering?*

When did all these rugged, no-nonsense guys become New Sensitive Men? Maybe Rather should have taken Eric Engberg and Andrew Heyward into the woods so they could all bang on their drums for a few hours to get over their *pain and suffering.*

When these poor guys weren't feeling their own pain, they were doing their best to inflict more on me.

Bob Schieffer, the chief Washington correspondent for CBS News, told the *Washington Post,* "It's such a wacky charge, and a weird way to go about it. . . . I don't know what Bernie was driving at. It just sounds bizarre."

Wacky? Weird? Bizarre? What I found wacky, weird, and bizarre was that the chief Washington CBS News correspondent found absolutely nothing wrong with Engberg's piece and was now saying that if I really thought there was a liberal bias at CBS News, then there was only one honorable thing for me to do: get the hell out!

"If this place is as ethically corrupt as he [Goldberg] seems to think, I think he'd have no alternative but to resign." Love it or leave it was Schieffer's brilliant advice.

Tom Brokaw, the NBC News anchor, joined the chorus. "It was inappropriate" for me to "go to a newspaper like the *Wall Street Journal* [and] attack your own organization," he said on CNBC.

I wondered what Brokaw would do if he found out that General Electric, the company that owns NBC and signs his paychecks, was ripping off consumers by making shoddy lightbulbs in order to rake in a few extra bucks. Would Tom think it was "inappropriate" to "attack" his own organization by going public with the story?

And I wondered what Tom would do if he learned that GE was making bad airplane engines? Where would *his* allegiance be: to his boss or to his viewers?

Back in 1996, when that question crossed my mind, it was nothing more than one of those hypothetical, what-if scenarios that I never expected would really happen.

But it did.

On January 2, 2001—five years after Tom bashed me for "attacking" my own organization, as he put it—the *Wall Street Journal* ran a lead story on page one reporting that federal safety officials were looking into problems with a certain GE airplane engine. They were worried that parts of the engines might disintegrate and someday cause a major air disaster.

After the story broke, GE confirmed that the *WSJ* got it substantially right, adding that the company was working hard to resolve any possible malfunctions on the engine, the CF6, which powers a variety of wide-bodied airplanes, including the 747, 767, and DC-10, as well as Air Force One and several models of the Airbus.

A GE spokesman said whatever problems there were "happened weeks and in some cases several months ago." Nonetheless, GE stock dropped nearly 9 percent in one day because of the news.

Sounds like a pretty big story to me. Possible problems with engines attached to more than four thousand airplanes that carry thousands of passengers every day. More than a dozen newspapers picked up the story right after it ran in the *Wall Street Journal*. And given the drop in the price of GE shares, CNBC, the cable business news channel, which is part of NBC and owned by GE, also ran the story. So how did Tom Brokaw play it on his nightly newscast? He didn't. He decided not to "attack" GE, his own organization.

I understand that a journalist has to be loyal to his own bosses, the people who sign the paychecks, but if there's a conflict, the viewer or the reader has to come first. In the long run, that's best for his news organization, too. That's what I thought, anyway, when I wrote the op-ed.

But while newspapers all over the country were writing about the furor my column had caused, the *New York Times*, the newspaper of record, did not see fit to print a single word about the issue I had raised. The world's most important newspaper, which would make room on page one for a story about the economy of Upper Volta or about the election of a lesbian dogcatcher in Azerbaijan or about affirmative action in Fiji, didn't think a story about media bias, leveled by a network news correspondent, was worth even a few paragraphs.

That, however, did not stop one of the paper's heaviest hitters, veteran political analyst R. W. "Johnny" Apple, from sounding off on television.

On CNN's *Reliable Sources*, Apple said, "There's no suggestion here that this man [Goldberg] went to CBS over a period of time and said, 'Our stuff is all one-sided, we've got to do something about this.'... There's no suggestion that he has done that. He has simply stabbed this guy [Engberg] in the back."

It's fun to watch someone as respected and thoughtful and pompous as Johnny Apple make a complete fool of himself. Being a windbag is one thing, but being a windbag on a worldwide television network is a sight to behold.

First of all, I never said, "Our stuff is all one-sided." That's not the nature of the bias problem. The problem is that bias pops up too often.

On Apple's other point—that I never discussed the problem in hopes of fixing it—how did Johnny Apple know I didn't go to CBS News with my concerns? Did he call me to find out? No, he didn't. The fact is, I had gone to CBS News over a very long period of time; I had in fact complained about our coverage; and if Apple had bothered to ask, I would have told him.

If making one phone call was too much work for Johnny Apple, he could have at least read the *Washington Post*, which I'm sure he sees every day since he's based in Washington himself. The *Post*'s media writer, Howard Kurtz, reported that "Goldberg has told friends he feels bad about hurting Engberg, but that he has complained to CBS management about a liberal tilt for several years and been consistently ignored."

None of this mattered. The media elites were circling the wagons. I could have shot a Christian Fundamentalist at an anti-abortion rally in Times Square at high noon, and they would have been more sympathetic than they were now that I had written about bias in the media.

"Bernie is certainly entitled to his political views," Andrew Heyward told John Carmody, who at the time wrote a media gossip column for the *Washington Post*, "and his politics have been known for a very long time."

The best I can figure is that I must have been in a coma the day I turned into the Rush Limbaugh of CBS News. But there it was, the president of CBS News telling the *Washington Post* that I was entitled to my "political views" and that my "politics have been known for a very long time."

What exactly were these political views that I had expressed in the op-ed column? Did I come out for Steve Forbes? Did I come out for his flat tax? On both counts the answer is no. I didn't defend the flat tax, and I didn't so much as imply that Steve Forbes might make a good president.

So what political views had I expressed? That the media elites have a liberal bias? Couldn't an honest, nonpartisan observer who cares about his own news organization come to that conclusion? I guess not—at least not as far as CBS News was concerned.

Maybe I should have seen the humor in the whole thing. I was pointing fingers at the media elites, which only proved to them that *I* was the one who had a bias problem. Wasn't this what used to happen—on a much scarier and devastating scale, for sure—in the old Soviet Union? A dissident says the elites are corrupt, so the elites throw him in the Gulag because his accusation proves beyond any doubt . . . *that the dissident is insane.*

By this point, it had become painfully clear that Dan Rather and the CBS News brass were not going to let bias be the issue. They were making *me* the issue. It didn't take much courage for Rather and his band of Lilliputians to smack me down, because I couldn't fight back—and they knew it. If I had even tried, I have no doubt CBS would have fired me on the spot!

So I didn't go to the newspapers and say, "Does Dan Rather really think the piece about Forbes and his flat tax was fair and objective journalism?

"Does Dan think it's okay for one of his Washington reporters to marginalize a presidential candidate and do David Letterman Top Ten jokes about his biggest issue? Does that meet Dan's standard of fairness?

"Does Andrew Heyward plan more pieces that refer to the centerpiece of a candidate's presidential campaign as 'wacky.'"

I couldn't say anything.

I took all of Bob Schieffer's shots without ever saying, "What's wacky, weird, and bizarre is that Bob Schieffer, who ought to know better, is deaf, dumb, and blind when it comes to spotting an editorial passing itself off as straight news."

But I knew that I had gotten myself into this mess—not by expressing an opinion that Rather and the others would hate—*but by putting my name on the opinion.* I could have gone to a dozen newspaper reporters who write about television and suggested they get a tape of the Engberg piece, and then blast it—"off the record." I could have said all the things I said in the *Wall Street Journal* column and a lot more, *without using my name.*

Guys like Rather, Schieffer, and Heyward operate that way all the time.

When Dan wanted to get rid of his evening news coanchor, Connie Chung, because he felt she was getting uppity by demanding more airtime, he and his friends ripped her to shreds in the press—*but you rarely saw his name attached to the story.*

When the *CBS Evening News* sent Connie to Oklahoma City on April 19, 1995—*before they sent Dan in, who was on vacation*—to anchor one of the biggest stories of our time, the bombing of the Alfred P. Murrah Federal Building and the death of 168 innocent people, Dan was so incensed that Connie was on the air first and getting all the airtime that when he finally arrived in Oklahoma City, he spent hours and hours on the phone with TV writers, blasting Connie Chung as a second-rate journalist.

Several CBS news people heard him do it. "Dan was behind a curtain [in the makeshift CBS newsroom at the CBS affiliate in Oklahoma City] ripping her," one of them told me. "He was on the phone for hours blasting her." Of course, he wasn't speaking "on the record," so you couldn't find his name in any of the stories. Just one month later, when Connie was dumped from CBS News, Dan did go on the record and was quoted by name, in the *Boston Globe Magazine*, saying of his former coanchor: "I'm a friend of hers. I was yesterday, I am today, and I will be tomorrow." Boy, did that sound familiar.

This was Dan speaking pure Dan-ish. "I'm a friend of hers" means "I am *not* a friend of hers." "I was [her friend] yesterday, I am today, and I will be tomorrow" means "I'm glad they finally fired her so I can have more airtime for myself."

This is the ugly, take-no-prisoners side of Dan that comes out when he feels threatened. It's as if he doesn't understand how big and important he has become over the years, how far he's traveled from the small-town, blue-collar, Depression-era Texas of his childhood. It's as if he doesn't know that he can afford to be generous.

One hundred sixty-eight human beings, including nineteen children, are blown to smithereens and Dan—anonymously—is miffed because Connie Chung is getting more airtime than he is! But Dan left no fingerprints. At least I had the guts to attach my name to what I believed.

And I thought it was amusing, in a perverse kind of way, that the president of CBS News, Andrew Heyward, never said that the charge of liberal bias at CBS News and the other networks was a pathetic fabrication of my supposed right-wing imagination and was utterly ludicrous and without merit.

There was a reason for this. While Andrew was shouting to the *Washington Post* that my "politics had been known for a very long time," he was whispering something quite different, privately.

"The Emperor Is Naked" 3

When the magazine show *Eye to Eye* with Connie Chung first started up in 1993, I went to Heyward, who was then the show's executive producer, with an idea.

"Let's do a piece about whether there really is a liberal bias in television news," I said in his office on West 57th Street in Manhattan.

I told Heyward I would put in requests to interview Rather and Brokaw and Jennings. I'd put responsible critics on, too. People who believed there was a leftward tilt to the news. The report I envisioned would be fair and balanced, just the way the news was supposed to be at CBS. Since this was the one topic that pretty much had been out of bounds on network news, I thought it might create a buzz and spark some interest in our new magazine show.

If Heyward were hooked up to a machine that measured his enthusiasm level, the needle wouldn't have budged. If, on the other hand, I had suggested a story about serial killers who murder prostitutes or little girls who kill their baby-sisters—stories Heyward actually put on

Eye to Eye—the needle would have been dancing all over the place. But a story about bias in the news? A story that might offend The Dan? Heyward probably thought I was high on drugs to even mention it.

But I persisted, telling Andrew that we do stories about everything else, about every other institution in America; why not a story about ourselves? He gave an inch. Heyward said he would talk to Eric Ober, then the president of CBS News, and see what he thought.

A few days later Heyward came back with the answer. Ober wasn't enthusiastic either. But, he said, there might be a middle ground. I could do the story, he said, "but you can't ask Dan any tough questions." At first I thought he was kidding. *You can't ask Dan any tough questions?* Heyward has a dry sense of humor. When has an executive producer or a news president *ever* said a reporter *can't* ask somebody tough questions? A reporter would be in hot water if he or she *didn't* ask tough questions on a controversial issue.

Can you imagine if I said I wanted to do a profile of Rush Limbaugh and Heyward said, *"Okay, but you can't ask Rush any tough questions"*?

Or Newt Gingrich. *"Sure, Bernie, you can do a piece, but make sure you don't ask him any tough questions."*

"You have got to be kidding," I said to Heyward. "You can't possibly be serious!" Heyward said he was not kidding and that he was serious.

Now it was my turn to say I didn't want any part of this story. Not with these ridiculous restrictions. Dan was not the bad guy. Not directly anyway. Heyward and Ober never asked how he'd feel about such a story. They just knew.

Everyone is afraid of crossing The Dan, who, Sicilian style, divides the world into friends and enemies. And you don't want to be caught on the wrong side of the line. Ober and Heyward and a lot of others put Rather's concerns—or their notion of his concerns—before the concerns of their viewers, who, I still think, would have respected us more, not less, for doing a tough, honest story about ourselves.

Rather's baby-sitters were coddling him as if he were Ted Baxter, a smiling fool who didn't know enough about his own business to answer a few tough questions. This was unfair to Dan, who speaks reasonably and articulately all the time about the news business. Couldn't he make a case that the bias charges were bogus? His handlers weren't about to find out by putting Dan Rather in the very same hot seat he had put so many people in during his career. They felt they had to protect him from "tough questions." They had to protect CBS News, and the other networks, too, from—what?—a ten-minute magazine story that would raise the question: Is there a liberal bias in network television news?

What were they so afraid of?

There was one other thing Andrew Heyward told me, face to face, in his *Eye to Eye* office. It was something that would haunt me a few years later when I was twisting in the wind for writing my op-ed column.

"Look, Bernie," he said, "of course there's a liberal bias in the news. All the networks tilt left." He said it in such a way as to indicate, "Come on, we all know it—*the whole damn world knows it*—but that doesn't mean we have to put it on the air!"

And Heyward said one other thing I will always remember: "If you repeat any of this, I'll deny it."

Three years after that conversation in Andrew's office, in February of 1996 when my op-ed piece came out, Heyward was still trying to balance what he knew privately to be true with what he felt he could say publicly. There were other considerations, practical issues that had to be taken into account. If he had acknowledged that I might be onto something—even if my decision to go public was something he deplored—Heyward would have his hands full with Rather and Schieffer and Engberg and a lot of others at CBS News.

So Heyward told the *Washington Post*: "Was he [Goldberg] acting on principle? Yes. Was he a misguided missile? Yes." He knew I wasn't trying to hurt anyone. He knew, from hundreds of conversations over many years, how much I cared about journalism at CBS News.

Publicly, Heyward said that what I had done was "a real hand grenade thrown among his colleagues," that it was "a real breach of our fundamental trust."

But privately the president of CBS News was saying something else altogether. Privately, he told me the Engberg piece represented "a conspiracy of fuck-ups," because no one had stopped it before it got on the air. What he didn't say, not explicitly anyway, was that they let it on the air *precisely* because they didn't see anything wrong with it.

Andrew knew the Engberg piece was indefensible, but he would never say so publicly. If he had, I wouldn't have been so alone and isolated.

In the halls at CBS News New York the day the op-ed came out, many colleagues shunned me. They averted their eyes as if I had some kind of fatal disease. Al Ortiz, then the Washington bureau chief and Engberg's immediate boss, called and, in a very polite and gentlemanly way, asked, "What in the world were you thinking when you wrote that piece?"

What in the world was I thinking? Did you ever wonder, Al, even for one damn second, what in the world your own correspondent, Eric Engberg, was thinking? Did you wonder what in the world your producers in Washington were thinking when they edited the piece and sent it on to New York?

I thought it, but didn't say it, because there was no point in making even more enemies than I already had. So I told Ortiz that I meant no personal harm to Engberg or Rather or anyone else. My intent was to get a discussion going, because, until now, no one took my complaints about bias seriously.

Then I asked Ortiz a question: "What did *you* think of Engberg's piece?" Ortiz said he "winced" when Engberg referred to Forbes's "Number One Wackiest Flat-Tax Promise." The Washington bureau manager "*winced.*" And then he did absolutely nothing.

While the heat was being turned up inside the Broadcast Center in New York, something quite different was happening on the outside. It's as if there were two Americas, or at least two American cultures: the media-elite America, which was shunning me, and the other America— the one between Manhattan and Malibu—which was thanking and congratulating me for saying publicly what they had been thinking for years.

Over the next few weeks I received hundreds of letters (some of which are reproduced in Appendix B) and phone calls, a few from fellow journalists, but the overwhelming majority from regular Americans whose only contact with the big-time media is when they turn on their TV sets to watch the evening news. It was these people who helped me understand that no matter how I was being treated inside CBS News, no matter how alien my views were in-house, outside I had many supporters who were actually grateful for what I had written.

I heard from a man named Joseph Doyle, of Waynesboro, Pennsylvania, who wrote: "I wish to join with so many other Americans in thanking you for raising such a very important issue. I find it incredible that Andrew Heyward, CBS News Division President, chooses to treat you as the issue rather than the liberal bias of the media elites."

Herbert Russell of Carbondale, Illinois, wrote: "Liberal bias among the television networks has done something that market forces could not have engendered, the revitalization of radio. Rush Limbaugh would never have become the success he has if the firm of Rather, Brokaw, and Jennings had done its job. Instead, they failed."

Jan McDonough of Fort Worth, Texas, wrote: "Those of us outside the media have been aware for years of the liberal bias that is so pervasive. That's why the 'alternative' media audience has grown and the so-called 'mainstream' media audience is shrinking."

Richard Asper, from Watertown, South Dakota, noticed that CBS News had taken me off the air. So he sent me a letter that asked: "Where are you? Since you wrote that op-ed piece for the *Wall Street Journal* exposing the media's liberal bias, it's like you disappeared. Never fear, I have an idea!"

His idea was to include in his letter a drawing of a milk carton, with a space right in the middle for my picture. Beneath the milk carton, he had written:

"Have you seen this man?

"Name: Bernard Goldberg.

"Subject has been missing since he told the truth about the media's liberal bias.

"We fear the worst."

I also heard from a few brave souls in the media. John Stossel, the iconoclastic ABC News correspondent, called from an airplane to say he thought the op-ed piece was "right on the money."

An especially courageous producer at *60 Minutes*, whose name I won't mention to protect her from possible repercussions, left a voice mail saying, "I agree with your premise and am proud to tell anybody that I do." She also said the op-ed piece was "being hotly discussed in the halls here [at *60 Minutes*] and I must tell you that [there are] those in management who won't go on the record but agree with your premise as well. Hang in there."

A news director at a television station CBS owns (I won't use his name, either) wrote to say, "I can't figure out people who claim to love journalism but when someone comes along and points out something that needs attention, they can't handle it."

Roger Ailes of Fox News called with an especially elegant message: "You got balls, Goldberg."

Dick Wolf, the executive producer of the NBC show *Law & Order*, left a voice mail that said: "That was a hell of a piece in the *Wall Street Journal*. I agree with every single comma and semicolon in it. You were one thousand percent on the money. It was great to say that 'Yes indeed, the Emperor is naked.'"

Bob Costas, the NBC and HBO star who is one of the most thoughtful people in all of television, and who is a friend, left a message saying, "My guess is this [answering] machine is filled to the point of near explosion.... Buck up, if in fact you need bucking up, because what you did, essentially, is just in keeping with who you want to be and who you should be."

Peter Boyer—former media writer at the *New York Times* and the *New Yorker* and author of *Who Killed CBS*—sent me a heartwarming letter that said, in part, "I cannot guess what interior politics preceded it, and shudder to imagine what followed, but your WSJ column today was one righteous piece of commentary.... If I may presume to say so, CBS News should be proud."

Then I opened an interoffice envelope and on bright yellow paper was a short note from a CBS News colleague.

"In the future, if you have any derogatory remarks to make about CBS News or one of your co-workers.... I hope you'll do the same thing again."

It was signed, "Regards, Andy Rooney."

Identity Politics 4

I **grew up in a blue-collar,** Democratic family in the South Bronx. We lived in a tenement that was old even back then.

My father, Sam, worked long hours at a factory where they put embroidery on fabrics, everything from tablecloths to dresses.

My mother, Sylvia, took care of things at home, mostly my two brothers and me.

My elementary school, P.S. 61, was on Charlotte Street, an old, rundown couple of blocks that (long after I was gone) caught the attention of both Jimmy Carter and Ronald Reagan. Both had traipsed through the neighborhood, camera crews in tow, because, by the time they discovered it, Charlotte Street was widely seen as one of the most rundown slums in all of America, a national symbol of urban decay.

My parents had to cash in a small insurance policy to get me started in college, another public school, Rutgers University in New Brunswick, New Jersey. At Rutgers, like most of us on campus in the 1960s, I was liberal on all the big issues. I was an especially big fan of Lyndon Johnson's Great Society.

I thought then, and still do today, that Martin Luther King is one of the two or three greatest and most courageous Americans of the twentieth century.

I didn't vote for Reagan either time. But I did vote for McGovern— twice. Once in the Florida primary and again in the 1972 general election.

I'm pro-choice, with reservations, especially when it comes to minors. And I'm for gay rights, too.

Not exactly the credentials of some raging right-winger or even some country-club Republican.

By way of full disclosure, I admit I had a flirtation with conservatism in my younger days. When I was a little kid growing up in the Bronx in the 1950s, I was a die-hard Yankee fan, but I swear that's the closest I've ever come to openly supporting the military-industrial complex or anything so blatantly right-wing!

I know they used to say that rooting for the Yankees was like rooting for General Motors, but that doesn't *necessarily* make me a Republican, does it? Ira Glasser, the card-carrying, former executive director of the American Civil Liberties Union, once wrote that "it was the Yankee fans who grew up to believe in oil depletion allowances." Hey, I was seven years old! The only allowance I cared about was the twenty-five cents a week my parents gave me. Nonetheless, I do admit that on more than one occasion I did in fact sit in the bleachers at Yankee Stadium, eating hot dogs and drinking Cokes, and generally living it up with all those other rotten capitalists.

Sue me!

These days, like most Americans, I'm still against racial discrimination. I'd even make it a *criminal* offense, not just civil. But I'm against it even when its targets are white people. So while I'm for what we like to call affirmative action when that means reaching out to bring more minorities into the process, I'm against affirmative action when it means racial preferences, which in the real world is what affirmative action is usually about. Why should the children of Jesse Jackson or Colin Powell or Diana Ross get some kind of racial preference when they apply to college or go out for a job, but no "affirmative action" is given to the child of a white Anglo-Saxon Protestant coal miner from West Virginia?

I'm also against affirmative action for "legacies"—kids, almost always white, who get accepted by a college because mommy or daddy went there twenty-five years earlier.

I'm also 100 percent against sex discrimination, just as I was when the modern women's movement began in the 1960s and early 1970s. But these days I see an awful lot of sexism masquerading as feminism. Which means I'm against sex discrimination even when it's aimed at men, whether it's called affirmative action or anything else.

I also think there's too much male bashing in our culture—too many TV shows that demean men in general and fathers in particular and too many professional feminists who see men as dumb jerks who "just don't get it."

I think welfare is absolutely necessary for some people, but I also think it's wrecked the lives of far too many Americans who have gotten hooked on it.

If all that makes me a neoconservative, fine. But I see myself as an old-fashioned liberal. I'm a liberal the way liberals *used to be.*

My views these days are fairly mainstream in our country. But not in America's newsrooms. Which helps explain why, after I wrote the *WSJ* column, Dan started suggesting I was a "political activist" with a "special political agenda."

I started working at the Associated Press in New York City four days after I graduated from Rutgers in 1967. I was earning the princely sum of $102.50 a week, and I never spent a second thinking about media bias.

In 1969 I moved to Miami to work at WTVJ, then the local CBS television affiliate. That's about the time that Vice President Agnew started giving alliteration a bad name. Members of the national press were a bunch of "nattering nabobs of negativism," because of the grief they were giving Nixon over the war in Vietnam. The words may have come from William Safire's typewriter, but the enthusiasm and zest were Agnew's.

I guess I thought about what Agnew was saying—*for about a second*—before I dismissed it. I didn't take Spiro Agnew seriously. (And neither, apparently, did Richard Nixon. John Ehrlichman, one of Nixon's palace guards, wrote in his memoir, *Witness to Power*, that the president used to joke that "No assassin in his right mind would kill me. They know if they did that they would wind up with Agnew!")

In 1972, CBS News hired me and assigned me to the network news bureau in Atlanta.

I was still in high school and college at the height of the 1960s civil rights story, but I managed to cover the 1970s version in the South. I witnessed things up close I had only seen on television before.

To this day, I can see the Atlanta police on their horses, swinging batons at black civil rights demonstrators whose one and only crime was that they had no formal permit to march. The demonstration had started late one afternoon on Auburn Street, at the Ebenezer Baptist Church, where Martin Luther King Jr. and his father had preached, and was heading for downtown Atlanta about a mile away.

My camera crew and I were walking with the demonstrators. Everything was peaceful and then, in the blink of an eye, the police came out of nowhere. They had been hiding a few blocks ahead, behind some buildings. The marchers kept moving downtown, and the police came riding up, right at them. When the marchers wouldn't stop, the police, most of them white, rode in circles around the demonstrators, almost all of them black, swinging their nightsticks at anyone who got in the way.

That leaves an impression on a young reporter, especially one who grew up liberal in the North.

I covered George Wallace before and after he was shot. I worked with good-ol'-boy camera crews who liked the message Wallace was sending to America. I got into more than a few verbal brawls with them over how in the world they could admire this man who once promised "segregation today, segregation tomorrow, segregation forever" during one of his campaigns for governor of Alabama.

During the oil boycott of the early 1970s, I met a truly vile man named J. B. Stoner, a bigot of world-class proportions, who years later would be convicted of dynamiting a black church in Birmingham, Alabama.

I found Stoner's name in the diary of the man who had kidnapped an Atlanta newspaper editor named Reg Murphy. This came not long after Patricia Hearst was kidnapped in California. So it was a pretty big story.

I went to Stoner's house in Marietta, Georgia, to see what he might have to say. But my camera crew and I couldn't get to the front door, which was being protected by a pacing, barking, worked-up German shepherd behind a fence. When Stoner came out, my cameraman, John Smith, a southerner born and bred, had the good sense to do the talking.

"Mr. Stoner," he said, thickening up the accent just a tad to smooth the way, "my name is John Smith. I'm with CBS News. And this is Leroy Rollins, my sound man." Leroy was another good ol' white boy from the Deep South, who, like Smith, shook Stoner's hand. "And Mr. Stoner," Smith went on, "this is Bernie . . ."—and at this point, Smith moved his hand across his mouth so that J. B. Stoner could not make out my last name.

Smith was a genius! Why offend this racist piece of garbage by letting him know there was a *Goldberg* on his property. *"This is Bernie mumble mumble mumble . . ."* Brilliant!

After we talked outside in his yard for a while, pretty much getting nowhere on the kidnap story, Stoner went back in to get a little memento he thought we might like. It was a bumper sticker that represented Stoner's philosophy on the oil crisis. He brought three of them out, one for each of his new buddies. The slogan was: "Oil Yes—Jews No."

There was real bias in our culture back then, but I can't remember seeing bias in the news. I was in my twenties, and these were some of the new experiences that were shaping my life. I loved the idea that my stories were on a newscast anchored by the most trusted man in America, Walter Cronkite. Maybe I was too busy running all over the place covering tornadoes and train wrecks and southern pols and civil rights demonstrations, but media bias was not on my radar screen. I don't remember talking about it or thinking about it except when Nixon and Agnew brought it up, and then, as I say, given their not-so-hidden agenda, I dismissed it.

The 1980s, however, were a completely different story.

These were the Reagan Years. His campaign ads said it was "Morning in America," which was a Madison Avenue way of conjuring up images of something fresh and tranquil settling over the landscape. This would not be the turbulent and psychedelic 1960s or the dark and gloomy 1970s. The 1980s, the Reagan Years, would be when we returned to Norman Rockwell's America.

Ronald Reagan said all the things the majority of Americans wanted to hear. That we pay too much taxes. That the Soviet Union was an Evil Empire. That it was time to restore traditional Family Values to America.

Liberals were gagging from sea to shining sea.

There was one thing Reagan did not talk about—the disease that had just begun ravaging gays from San Francisco to New York. AIDS.

To the Liberal Establishment, Ronald Reagan was a Neanderthal. He was old, he wasn't hip, and, worst of all, they saw him as stupid, "an amiable dunce," to use the put-down of choice.

To the Left, Reagan was no more than a two-bit actor who was merely reading the words that the smarter and scarier right-wingers had put in front of him. Liberals saw him as an insensitive old man who would rather spend money on missiles than on new schoolhouses.

To feminists on the Left, he was the symbol of the oppressive white male power structure.

To gays, he was the reason AIDS was spreading.

To blacks, he was the president who ridiculed "welfare queens."

There was something in the Reagan Revolution for every liberal to hate.

(In fairness, years later, some liberals in the media changed their minds about Reagan, no longer portraying him as a simpleton. On September 9, 1999, for instance, *Newsweek*'s assistant managing editor Evan Thomas—whose grandfather Norman ran for president of the United States six times as a socialist—generously offered up this appraisal of the former president, on a nationally syndicated TV talk show called *Inside Washington*: "He had kind of an intuitive idiot genius," Thomas said, referring to Mr. Reagan's contribution to bringing down the Soviet empire. To some media elites, like Evan Thomas, who went to Andover and Harvard, Ronald Reagan had evolved all the way from a plain old simple idiot . . . to an idiot genius. How nice.)

It was in this atmosphere that liberals felt as if they were on the outside looking in, which they were. They felt as if they were under siege. And they became very sensitive to every slight, real or imagined.

Political correctness started to take hold. Jokes about how many feminists it took to change a lightbulb weren't funny, damn it! Any suggestion from straight Americans that gays might actually be fueling the AIDS epidemic with reckless behavior, by refusing, for instance, to shut down bathhouses that celebrated gay, anonymous, orgy-like sex, was seen as homophobia. Anyone who argued against affirmative action ran the risk of being called a racist.

America was becoming balkanized. *E Pluribus Unum*—From Many, One—was being turned on its head.

And the national news media, print and TV, were not just covering this important trend in American culture. They were taking sides.

In 1981, having worked out of CBS News bureaus in Atlanta and then San Francisco, I was named a national correspondent, which allowed me to cover bigger, more important stories anywhere in the country. My new base was CBS News headquarters in New York, where I was assigned to the evening news and its brand-new anchor, Dan Rather, who had just replaced Walter Cronkite.

It was in New York that for the first time I started noticing things that made me feel uneasy.

I noticed that we pointedly identified conservatives as conservatives, for example, but for some crazy reason didn't bother to identify liberals as liberals.

Harry Smith, the cohost (at the time) of *CBS This Morning*, introduced a segment on sexual harassment saying: "... has anything really changed? Just ahead we're going to ask noted law professor Catharine MacKinnon and conservative spokeswoman Phyllis Schlafly to talk about that."

It sounds innocent enough, but why is it that Phyllis Schlafly was identified as a conservative, but Catharine MacKinnon was not identified as a radical feminist or a far-left law professor or even as a plain old liberal? MacKinnon, after all, is at least as far to the left as Schlafly is to the right. Why was she simply a "noted law professor"? The clear implication was that Catharine MacKinnon is an objective, well-respected observer and Phyllis Schlafly is a political partisan.

In fact, during the Clarence Thomas–Anita Hill hearings, NBC News actually brought MacKinnon in as an "expert" to bring perspective to the hearings. MacKinnon is the feminist ideologue who had famously implied that all sexual intercourse is rape. This did not deter NBC News.

This blindness, this failure to see liberals as anything but middle-of-the-road moderates, happens all the time on network television. The Christian Coalition is identified as a conservative organization—so far, so good—but we don't identify the National Organization for Women (NOW) as a liberal organization, which it surely is.

Robert Bork is the "conservative" judge. But Laurence Tribe, who must have been on the *CBS Evening News* ten million times in the 1980s (and who during the contested presidential election in 2000 was a leading member of Team Gore, arguing the vice president's case before the U.S. Supreme Court), is identified simply as a "Harvard law professor." But Tribe is not *simply* a Harvard law professor. He's easily as liberal as Bork is conservative.

If we do a Hollywood story, it's not unusual to identify certain actors, like Tom Selleck or Bruce Willis, as conservatives. But Barbra Streisand or Rob Reiner, no matter how active they are in liberal Democratic politics, are just Barbra Streisand and Rob Reiner.

Rush Limbaugh is the *conservative* radio talk show host. But Rosie O'Donnell, who while hosting a fund-raiser for Hillary Clinton said Mayor Rudy Giuliani was New York's "village idiot," is not the *liberal* TV talk show host.

During the Clinton impeachment trial in 1999, as the senators signed their names in the oath book swearing they would be fair and impartial, Peter Jennings, who was anchoring ABC News's live coverage, made sure his audience knew which senators were *conservative*—but uttered not a word about which ones were *liberal*.

As the senators each signed the oath book, Jennings identified several Democrats, including Barbara Boxer and Ted Kennedy, two of the most liberal members of the Senate, without ever mentioning that they are indeed liberal. That would have been just fine, except for what happened later. When Senator John McCain signed the book, Jennings said, "Senator John McCain here of Arizona, left-hander. More right than left in his politics and intending to run for president of the United States."

Jennings spotted another conservative. "Senator McConnell of Kentucky, very determined conservative member of the Republican Party."

When Jennings identified the next senator to sign the book it was, "Senator Mikulski of Maryland."

Plain and simple. Unadorned. Senator Mikulski of Maryland. Not a word that Senator Mikulski is a liberal Democrat from Maryland.

Then, a few seconds later, Jennings, with pinpoint precision, continued identifying the conservatives. "Senator Rick Santorum, one of the younger members of the Senate, Republican, very determined conservative member of the Senate. That's Senator Daschle there in the left-hand side of your picture."

Santorum was a conservative Republican but Tom Daschle, a liberal from South Dakota, was simply... Senator Daschle.

Charles Schumer, the newly elected liberal senator from New York, was "Senator Schumer"... no label needed. But the next senator to sign the oath book was "Mr. Smith of New Hampshire, also another very, very conservative Republican intending to run for the presidency."

When Paul Wellstone of Minnesota and Ron Wyden of Oregon came up to sign—two more from the left wing of the Democratic Party—Jennings simply identified them by name and state. The word liberal never passed through Peter's lips. In fact, Peter felt no need to identify any of the Democratic liberals in the Senate. Not a single one. Only the conservative Republicans.

There's a better chance that Peter Jennings, the cool, sophisticated Canadian, would identify Mother Teresa as "the old broad who used to work in India" than there is that he would call a liberal Democrat... *a liberal Democrat!*

On that particular day, Peter identified the conservatives because he thought it mattered. He thought his viewers needed to know. And he was right. He didn't identify the liberals, obviously because he thought it didn't matter. And he was wrong.

In the world of the Jenningses and Brokaws and Rathers, conservatives are out of the mainstream and need to be identified. Liberals, on the other hand, *are* the mainstream and don't need to be identified.

I found out just how true that was during my last conversation with Dan, the one on the phone the day before the op-ed came out. That I would write such treasonous material was bad enough in Dan's eyes, but that I picked the *Wall Street Journal*—such a conservative paper— annoyed him too, and he let me know it.

"What do you call the *New York Times* editorial page?" I asked him, since he had written op-eds for that paper.

"Middle of the road," he said without missing a beat.

"You don't think the *New York Times* has a liberal editorial page?" I asked him, not believing what I had just heard.

"No," he said, "middle of the road."

This is a newspaper that consistently editorializes in favor of affirmative action, of all sorts of abortion rights, of strict gun-control laws, and is against the death penalty. The editorials are well written and well reasoned. But they do represent liberal points of view.

This is a newspaper that has endorsed for president Al Gore, Bill Clinton twice, Michael Dukakis, Walter Mondale, Jimmy Carter twice, George McGovern, Hubert Humphrey, Lyndon Johnson, and John Kennedy. You would have to go back to Dwight Eisenhower to find the last time the *New York Times* came out in favor of anyone even vaguely resembling a conservative.

And Dan Rather calls its editorial page "middle of the road."

This is the essence of the problem. To Dan Rather and to a lot of other powerful members of the chattering class, that which is right of center is conservative. That which is left of center is middle of the road. No wonder they can't recognize their own bias.

Why is it that the word "left-wing" has virtually vanished from the media's vocabulary? "Right-wing," on the other hand, is doing quite well, thank you. We have right-wing Republicans and right-wing Christians and right-wing Miami Cubans and right-wing radio talk show hosts.

Isn't *anybody* left-wing anymore?

Aren't there *any* left-wing Christians? Aren't Jesse Jackson and Senator Barbara Boxer and Congressman Barney Frank way out there on the left wing of the Democratic Party? Why is it that just about the only time you hear the term "left-wing" on a network evening newscast is when the anchors and reporters are talking about the part of an airplane that caught fire right before the crash?

Conservatives think this is proof that there's a dark conspiracy among the liberal media elites. They're wrong. I have never heard a single reporter or producer or anchor or executive say anything like: *Let's leave off the liberal label so we can make so-and-so appear high-minded and objective. And while we're at it, let's make sure we identify the other side as conservative so our viewers will know he or she is a partisan with a right-wing ideological ax to grind.*

It never happens that way. Never. Not even with a wink and a nod. If it did, we'd be a lot better off. Because *that* is fixable. *That* is blatant bias that cannot and would not be tolerated. What happens in reality is far worse.

The reason we don't identify NOW as a liberal group or Laurence Tribe as a liberal professor or Tom Daschle as a liberal Democrat is that, by and large, the media elites don't see them that way. It may be hard to believe, but liberals in the newsroom, pretty much, see NOW and Tribe and even left-wing Democrats as middle of the road. Not coincidentally, just as they see themselves. When you get right down to it, liberals in the newsroom see liberal views as just plain . . . *reasonable.*

No need to identify Patricia Ireland as head of a *liberal* women's group, because to the media elites her views are not leftist. They simply make sense. They're simply reasonable. After all, she's for abortion rights without restrictions, isn't she? She's for affirmative action, isn't she?

To mainstream America, these are major elements of the liberal agenda. But to the liberals in the media, these aren't liberal views at all. They're just sensible, reasonable, rational views, *which just happen to coincide with their own.*

I once asked Susan Zirinksy, a first-rate journalist who had been the *CBS Evening News* senior producer in Washington (she's now executive producer of *48 Hours*), how many times she went to conservative women's groups for on-camera reactions either to Supreme Court decisions or to votes in Congress regarding women's issues. She thought about it for a few seconds, then told me she couldn't think of a single time. In retrospect, even she found that odd.

I say "in retrospect" because at the time, she never gave it a second thought. Need a reaction? Go to NOW. What other group would you go to? Certainly not some "fringe" group that opposed abortion rights or affirmative action.

This is the kind of party-line thinking that prompted Michael Barone, the conservative Washington journalist, to say that the press is "one of America's most pro-feminist institutions."

But Zirinsky, who is an honest newswoman, never thought of it that way. She didn't act out of malice. She didn't conspire with anyone to freeze out conservative women. She just thought NOW was the logical place to go. NOW was the group that spoke for women. NOW wasn't a liberal group, to Zirinsky. It was a sensible, reasonable, and rational group.

Since conservative women like Phyllis Schlafly or conservative judges like Robert Bork have "unorthodox" views, *illiberal views*, we must make sure to identify them as conservatives so our audience won't think that they're objective—or worse, heaven forfend, that they're also sensible, reasonable, and rational.

If you hooked network news reporters and producers to polygraph machines and asked them, "Do you think you are guilty of liberal bias?" most would almost certainly answer, "No." And they would pass the polygraph test because they're not lying. They honestly believe what they're saying. And that's the biggest problem of all.

How Bill Clinton Cured Homelessness 5

In the 1980s, I started noticing that the homeless people we showed on the news didn't look very much like the homeless people I was tripping over on the sidewalk.

The ones on the sidewalk, by and large, were winos or drug addicts or schizophrenics. They mumbled crazy things or gave you the evil eye when they put paper coffee cups in your face and "asked" for money. Or they had drool coming down the side of their mouths and lived in cardboard boxes...but only until the spaceship came back to take them home to Planet Neutron.

But the ones we liked to show on television were different. They looked as if they came from your neighborhood and mine. They looked like us. And the message from TV news was that they didn't just *look* like us—they *were* like us! On NBC, Tom Brokaw said that the homeless are "people you know."

I'm sure Tom was right, even though, for some crazy reason, I personally didn't know *any* homeless people. Unless, of course, you count all those car-window washers on the street who, hoping for a buck or two, used to spit on my windshield at red lights because they ran out of Windex twenty years ago.

But many of the homeless that Tom and Dan and Peter showed on the nightly news were sympathetic souls who told stories about how, because of hard times, they were temporarily down on their luck. They reminded us of Tom Joad and his proud family in *The Grapes of Wrath*, who were brought down by the Depression. And I'm as guilty as the next reporter. Before I started showing the real homeless on the evening news, I made my bosses very happy by going to a soup kitchen in New York where I found a very atypical, blond-haired, blue-eyed family—husband, wife, kids . . . all that was missing was a dog named Rover—and put them on national television as the faces of homelessness in America. It was the only story like that I did; nonetheless, mea culpa.

They could have been any of us, the down-and-outers we showed. And that's exactly why they were on television so much, even though they made up only a tiny fraction of the homeless in America. In a word, we put them on TV for the reason television people do almost everything—*ratings*. Ratings are the God that network executives and their acolytes worship.

We know who our viewers are. We know what they look like. And we know that they would be drawn more to stories about homeless people who looked just like their mothers and fathers and sons and daughters than homeless people who looked like, well, homeless people.

But there was another, more insidious reason we focused on those people who looked like our next-door neighbors. If we journalists could win sympathy for *them*, then we had a chance of winning sympathy for the less sympathetic homeless, which might translate into a new homeless shelter—in some nonjournalist's neighborhood, of course.

But to do that we first needed to go to central casting and get just the right kind of homeless people on the news.

White was better than black. Clean was better than dirty. Attractive was better than unattractive. Sane was better than insane. And sober was better than addicted. So when the TV people went looking for just that right kind of homeless face to put on their news programs, they went to people like Robert Hayes, who ran the National Coalition for the Homeless in New York.

In 1989, Hayes told the *New York Times* that when congressional committees and TV news producers contact him, "they always want white, middle-class people to interview."

Walter Goodman, who writes about television for the *New York Times*, came up with a name for what we in the media were doing. He called it the "prettifying of reality."

> More often than not, a news story or documentary on the homeless will feature a hard-working, straight-living young couple or an attractive teen-ager and her child who have run into a spell of bad luck.
>
> The reasons for the choices are not obscure. If you want to arouse sympathy for the homeless, you do not put forward off-putting specimens. Television news producers can count on advocacy groups to supply them with model victims for viewing purposes, people who may even be untouched by the other afflictions discovered in . . . [a] survey of the homeless: mental illness, AIDS, domestic violence, and lack of education and skills. And why should a producer focus on one of the 50 percent of single homeless people who have served time in jail when he can just as easily find someone without a record?
>
> Whether the intention is to make a more moving show or build support for programs to help the homeless and possibly reassure viewers about having a small shelter in their neighborhood, the result is a prettifying of reality.

But it wasn't enough simply to prettify reality. We also had to exaggerate reality if we were really going to gain support and compassion for the homeless.

No one knows exactly how many homeless there were in America in the 1980s and early 1990s, but there were researched, educated estimates. For example, the U.S. Census Bureau figured it was about 230,000. The General Accounting Office of Congress put the number between 300,000 and 600,000. The Urban Institute said that there were somewhere between 355,000 and 462,000 homeless Americans. These numbers weren't state secrets. Reporters knew what they were. They just didn't care.

Meanwhile, the homeless lobby was putting the number of homeless in the millions. No matter how bad a problem really is, advocates think they need to portray it as worse. This is standard operating procedure with lobbies. Pump up the number of victims and we stand a better chance of getting more sympathy and support—more money—for our cause is what they correctly think.

We have come to expect this of advocates. They know their cause is worthy, so what harm can a little exaggeration do? But reporters—*when they also see the cause as worthy*—buy into it. They also become advocates. They take the numbers as gospel. They have no desire to look too deep, because if they do, God forbid, they might find something they'd rather not find. There's an old saying in the newsroom: Don't let the facts stand in the way of a good story!

So in 1989 on CNN, Candy Crowley, a fine, serious reporter, said that "winter is on the way and three million Americans have no place to call home."

Three million!

Not to be outdone, in January of 1993, Jackie Nespral, then the anchor of *NBC Weekend Today*, said, "nationally right now, five million people are believed to be homeless . . . and the numbers are increasing."

Five million!! And the numbers are increasing!!!

Charles Osgood of CBS News, one of the most talented journalists in all of broadcasting, reported, "It is estimated that by the year 2000, nineteen million Americans will be homeless unless something is done, and done now."

Nineteen million homeless by the turn of the century!!!!

And Ray Brady, one of the best in the business, who was reporting for the *CBS Evening News*, found homeless people who actually lived in homes. These were—ready for this?—the "hidden homeless."

Who are they? People who aren't homeless at all, but, because they can't afford their own places, are living at home with Mom and Dad, often in cushy houses in the suburbs with big-screen TVs and three squares a day.

It's as if our coverage of this very big story was being directed not by objective journalists but by the advocates for the homeless themselves. We took what they said at face value even though we would never do that with advocates for causes *we did not embrace.* Can we really imagine Rather, Brokaw, and Jennings simply passing along propaganda from the pro-life lobby? Or the anti–affirmative action crowd? Or the NRA? We would never try to build up sympathy for those causes or their supporters!

But advocates for the homeless misled us about all sorts of things— the number of homeless, who they were, why they were homeless—and because we embraced *their* cause, because we felt right at home on the homeless beat, we pretty much said, "Hey, no problem," and passed their misinformation on to the American people.

"Of all the lies that are swallowed and regurgitated by the media, the ones that hurt the most come from the Good Guys," Katherine Dunn wrote in the *New Republic* in 1993. "The grass-roots do-gooders, the social work heroes, the non-profit advocacy groups battling for peace, justice, and equality."

Who wants to get tough with people like that? They want to make things better, don't they? But "holding the good guys accountable," she wrote, "doesn't mean that they are bad guys. . . . Apply equal skepticism to both sides. And if your mother says she loves you, check it out."

In a story, groundbreaking for its candor, on May 22, 1989, Gina Kolata wrote on page one of the *New York Times* that "drug and alcohol abuse have emerged as a major reason for the homelessness of men, women, and families."

As my young daughter, Catherine, might put it . . . *Duhhh!*

It sounds so obvious now. But this was actually legitimate front-page news in 1989, because homeless advocates didn't like to talk about such things with reporters.

In that story, Robert Hayes revealed for the first time that homeless advocates like himself didn't tell reporters the whole truth because they feared the public would lose sympathy for the homeless. They misled reporters about how many of the homeless were also criminals. They misled the media about how many were addicts.

But Hayes said it was time to end the deception. "The bottom line," he said, "is that we have to tell the truth."

For years, the activists played the media as if they were part of the homeless PR machine. And reporters were more than willing to go along and be yanked around by the homeless lobby. A lot of news people, after all, got into journalism in the first place so they could change the world and make it a better place. Rallying support for the homeless was a golden opportunity. Besides, showing compassion makes us feel good about ourselves, which is no small point when you consider the abundance of narcissists who populate the world of television news.

When the "proper" victims are involved, we become journalist/social workers. And we live by the journalist/social worker motto: Afflict the comfortable and comfort the afflicted.

"Increasingly, journalists see themselves as society's designated saviors," Robert Lichter of the nonpartisan Center for Media and Public Affairs in Washington told me.

In the late 1980s, Lichter and his team analyzed 103 stories on the ABC, NBC, and CBS evening newscasts as well as twenty-six articles in *Time, Newsweek*, and *U.S. News & World Report*. The results, Lichter says, "provide a blueprint of advocacy journalism."

"Only one source in twenty-five," Lichter concluded, "blamed homelessness on the personal problems of the homeless themselves, such as mental illness, drug or alcohol abuse, or lack of skills or motivation. The other 96 percent blamed social or political conditions for their plight. The primary culprit cited was the housing market, including forces like high mortgage interest rates, high rents, downtown redevelopment, etc. Next in line was government inaction, especially the government's failure to provide adequate public housing."

To a lot of journalists in the press and TV, the villain was—who else?— Ronald Reagan, who in their view was the embodiment of the greedy 1980s. To them he was the typical archconservative, a politician who simply had no compassion for the homeless. As a matter of routine, they made it look as if the Reagan administration practically invented homelessness.

The media drumbeat was that Ronald Reagan's spending policies— not the pathologies of the homeless—were behind this terrible problem of homeless Americans.

On ABC News, John Martin reported on a rally in October 1989 in support of the homeless. "They came here to Washington from all over the country," Martin told his audience, "the rich, the famous, the ordinary, the down-and-out. They staged the biggest rally in behalf of the homeless since the Reagan Revolution forced severe cutbacks in government housing programs."

In a prime-time special on the 1980s in December 1989, Tom Brokaw said, "Reagan, as commander in chief, was the military's best friend. He gave the Pentagon almost everything it wanted." Then, with pictures of the homeless on the TV screen, Brokaw said, "Social programs? They suffered under Reagan. But he refused to see the cause and effect."

Garrick Utley, then of NBC News, reported in November 1990, "In the 1980s, the Reagan years, the amount of government money spent to build low-income housing was cut drastically. Then homelessness began to appear on streets and in doorsteps."

In the report that followed, Ed Rabel said, "During the Reagan years, according to the Congressional Budget Office, housing programs for the poor were slashed by billions of dollars: an 80 percent cut over eight years."

All of these reports were aired *after* the *New York Times*—the Holy Bible that TV journalists normally consult to find out not only *what* they should cover but *how* they should cover it—ran its front-page story that revealed the real culprit behind the homelessness problem was drug and alcohol abuse, not Ronald Reagan.

All of these TV reports came out *after* that story in the *Times* quoted Irving Shandler, who ran a rehabilitation center in Philadelphia, saying that "substance abuse is one of the major issues causing people to be homeless and keeping them homeless."

Did anyone, least of all seasoned reporters who pride themselves on their skepticism, really believe that the vast majority of the homeless— the addicted and the mentally ill—would virtually disappear from America's streets if only Ronald Reagan hadn't cut housing programs?

Scott Shuger, a Washington journalist who wrote a piece in the *Washington Monthly*—"Who Are the Homeless?"—certainly didn't. In a monument to common sense and politically incorrect wisdom, Shuger wrote, "There can be all the low-cost housing in the world and an untreated paranoid won't set foot in it, and an untreated schizophrenic might burn it down. . . . And a drug addict will spend the rent money on crack."

While economic factors, like affordable housing and jobs, are important, Shuger pointed out that other factors are even more important. "So homelessness is in large measure a mental health problem that defies the conventional liberal answers of housing and jobs," he wrote.

But on the evening newscasts, the drumbeat went on and on. It was Reagan who was to blame. While his tax cuts created a whole new class of ostentatiously rich Americans—yuppies with big expense accounts, big cigars, and even bigger limos—there was The Other America, where the homeless lived on the street and ate in soup kitchens, innocent victims of a conservative president's insensitivity.

It was a great story... even if it wasn't quite true. For reporters who were too young to cover the great civil rights struggle of the 1960s, the homeless story twenty years later was the next best thing.

In a December 1989 *Wall Street Journal* piece, Robert Lichter wrote, "The homeless story is becoming the 1980s counterpart of the 1960s civil rights story—a stark moral issue that calls for journalists to awaken the national conscience and force public action. The difficulty is that this advocacy approach can skew the depiction of the actual problem. And misperceptions born of good intentions are not the most promising basis for choosing the best ways to help the homeless."

In the end it didn't matter, because in the early 1990s a miracle descended upon the land. Homelessness disappeared. It was over. It no longer existed in the entire United States of America!

It was a fantastic story. A too-good-to-be-true story.

I know that homelessness ceased to exist because I watch television news. If homeless people still existed, Dan and Tom and Peter would have them all over the news. I mean, can you think of a better TV story than one showing poor, desperate homeless people begging for some loose change or sleeping in cardboard boxes... *in the bitter cold?*

I could be wrong, but I think homelessness ended the day Bill Clinton was sworn in as president. Which is one of those incredible coincidences, since it pretty much began the day Ronald Reagan was sworn in as president.

What are the odds?

So what gives? Why did network television and America's most important newspapers virtually stop covering homelessness in America, a story they were so in love with just a few years earlier?

Maybe reporters just got tired of the same old story after a decade. Those blond-haired, blue-eyed homeless families made for good TV— *but enough already!*

And those less savory, less attractive homeless people we eventually got around to showing on TV—when we weren't busy prettifying reality— the ones who had lost their minds after years of drug abuse and were now yelling at tormentors in the sky—they made for good TV, too. But after ten long years maybe even these strange people stopped entertaining us. We are, after all, a nation that gets bored easily. Everything—especially everything on television—*must* entertain us. Or else it must go.

Maybe journalist/social workers, along with the rest of America, simply were suffering from compassion fatigue, and after a decade of putting the homeless on TV, we finally got depressed with the whole bunch of them.

Maybe it was because, as Lee Stringer explains in his book *Grand Central Winter*, which chronicles his own homeless years living on the streets of New York City, "When the homeless ceased to be portrayed as blameless victims, people ceased to care. The image became one of people who just might have some complicity in their circumstances, and that changed the mood greatly."

Or maybe it was something else altogether. Maybe the critics on the right—who saw media conspiracies all over the place—were actually onto something this time. Did the media really discover homelessness because a Republican became president, only to forget it when a Democrat was elected?

Yes, according to Philip Terzian, an editor at the *Providence Journal* in Rhode Island, who worked in the administration of President Jimmy Carter.

In 1999 he wrote a column about the homeless and about a *Village Voice* study that showed that in 1988 the *New York Times* ran fifty stories on the homeless, including five on page one. But a decade later, in 1998, the *Times* ran only ten homeless stories, and none on page one. And since the networks take their cues from the *Times*, their coverage dropped off sharply, too. The conservative Media Research Center found that in 1990, when George Bush was president, there were seventy-one homeless stories on the ABC, CBS, NBC, and CNN evening newscasts. But in 1995, when Bill Clinton was in the White House, the number had gone down to just nine!

"The cynic in me has an obvious explanation," Terzian wrote. "In 1988, instead of a compassionate Democrat, there was a heartless Republican in the White House. Indeed, if you track press attention to homelessness, you will find a dramatic leap in coverage beginning in the early 1980s—when Ronald Reagan took office."

"The problem with homelessness," Terzian continued, "is that, for too long, it has been an issue of partisan convenience. It is not Republican spending policies that caused the explosion in homelessness but the progressive vision of closing down state mental institutions, the rise in drug and alcohol abuse, and the loss of any stigma attached to subsisting in the streets."

A few years earlier, in 1996, another "cynic," Andrew Peyton Thomas, wrote (in the notoriously conservative *Weekly Standard*): "The Right might well respond that the election of Bill Clinton made the [homeless] issue go away, since it was anti-Republican animus that brought the issue to life in the early 1980s."

I choose not to believe any of that. Instead, I choose to believe that the reason the press and TV did a million homeless stories during the

Reagan years and virtually none during the Clinton years is because there was a big homeless problem under Ronald Reagan and no homeless problem under Bill Clinton.

I also choose to believe that when the Sunday edition of *ABC World News Tonight* rediscovered the homeless story *just three weeks after George W. Bush was sworn in as president* it was nothing more than coincidence. That when reporter Bob Jamieson said, "In New York City the number of homeless in the shelter system has risen above twenty-five thousand a night *for the first time since the late 1980s*," it was not an attempt to say, "*Here we go again—a Republican is in the White House and the homeless are back.*" And on August 4, 2001, when CNN also rediscovered homelessness and quoted sources saying, "The number of homeless people is on the rise this summer," I choose to believe it was not CNN's way of suggesting that now that a conservative Republican is president, Reagan-era misery will soon be back with us in full force.

Instead I choose to believe homelessness really is a thing of the past and that we will not see a renewed interest in the homeless story just because Bill Clinton is gone and George W. Bush is in. I choose to believe the media would never play politics with poor homeless people. I choose to believe that Bill Clinton really did end homelessness and that the end of homelessness is good news. Fantastic news. I choose to believe it is too-good-to-be-true news.

Epidemic of Fear 6

Like most terrible human tragedies, AIDS was a great news story.

A mysterious virus comes out of nowhere and goes on a killing spree. Its earliest victims are mostly young gay men, who slowly, but all too surely, lose their strength and wither away. Sometimes they break out in purple splotches. In their final days they are skeletons. And then they die.

Where did the virus come from? Why did some people get it and not others? Could you "catch" it if someone sneezed on you? Could you get it from a kiss? What if you shook hands with someone who had AIDS—that kill you?

It didn't take long before the scientists discovered that HIV, the AIDS virus, was carried in blood and semen. That explained why its victims were mainly gay men who engaged in high-risk anal sex and junkies who shot drugs into their veins and shared "dirty" needles. In the early days, some got the disease from blood transfusions. Hemophiliacs were especially at risk.

By any imaginable standard, this should have been bad enough. These were human beings dying terrible deaths. What could be worse?

How about the possibility that this virus that was picking off junkies and gay men might start to spread to housewives in Des Moines and businessmen in Seattle?

How about the possibility that before long it wouldn't just be homosexual men at gay bars who would have to wonder if their next partner would be the one with the deadly virus? What if *everyone* who was having sex was playing Russian roulette?

It was a nightmare scenario. And it was exactly the story that AIDS activists desperately wanted to put out. The goal was simple: scare the hell out of straight America—then they would have to pay attention.

Otherwise, the activists feared, there would never be a national outcry over AIDS. Middle America would never get worked up enough—and neither would Congress or the president—to spend whatever it took to combat this modern-day plague. As long as the people dying were mostly gay men and junkies, the AIDS lobby had a problem.

The activists knew, instinctively, that Main Street America did not see these people as sympathetic characters. Junkies died every day, from overdoses and who knows what. So what if there was now a virus that was also killing them. The activists knew that America would never lose sleep over drug addicts dying from something called HIV.

And homosexuals? The gay lobby was convinced that straight Americans didn't care what happened to them, either. But if the activists somehow could persuade America that gays and junkies were only the first wave, that heterosexuals were next, then the nation surely would demand that the government put all its efforts into finding a cure or a vaccine—*anything!*—to combat this deadly disease.

But to do this, the activists needed their compassionate friends in the media.

No problem!

It was the homeless story all over again. Tell the American people there were AIDS victims just like themselves—if not right now, soon— then maybe they would care enough to do something about the problem. The battle cry was as clear as can be: *no one is safe anymore!*

Once again, the media were more than willing to set aside their usual skepticism and go right along. While AIDS was devastating minority and gay communities in America, while it was leaving Middle America virtually untouched, the news stories conjured up some other reality.

U.S. News & World Report said, "The disease of *them* is suddenly the disease of *us*."

USA Today ran a headline that said, "Cases Rising Fastest Among Heterosexuals."

Time reported: "The proportion of heterosexual cases . . . is increasing at a worrisome rate. . . . The numbers as yet are small, but AIDS is a growing threat to the heterosexual population."

The *Atlantic Monthly* headlined a cover story: "Heterosexuals and AIDS: The Second Stage of the Epidemic."

The *Ladies Home Journal* ran a story with this tease on the cover: "AIDS & Marriage: What Every Wife Must Know."

And in 1987, one of the most famous, beloved, and listened-to Americans of all weighed in with a warning about heterosexual AIDS.

"AIDS has both sexes running scared. Research studies now project that one in five—listen to me, hard to believe—one in five heterosexuals could be dead from AIDS at the end of the next three years. That's by 1990. One in five. It is no longer just a gay disease. Believe me."

Who wouldn't believe Oprah Winfrey? Especially about something so important. Especially when the federal government put up nearly five million dollars for an "AIDS Doesn't Discriminate" advertising campaign that focused mainly on the one group that wasn't in real danger: heterosexuals who were not having sex with junkies.

No wonder an epidemic was racing across America. An epidemic of fear. You couldn't open a newspaper, turn the page of a magazine, or tune in to the nightly news without reading or hearing about the deadly link between AIDS and heterosexuals. The hysteria was creating a generation, perhaps the first generation ever, to equate sex with death!

But you couldn't really blame the media, not at first, anyway. Not when so many authorities were feeding them the horror stories. Dr. Robert Redfield, an infectious disease specialist at Walter Reed Army Hospital in Washington, told the Associated Press in 1985, "This is a general disease now. Get rid of the high-risk groups, anyone can get it."

In 1987 the highly respected surgeon general, C. Everett Koop, said AIDS was "the biggest threat to health this nation has ever faced."

Despite evidence to the contrary—heterosexuals were not falling by the wayside like junkies or gay men—the press, especially TV, loved the "No One Is Safe Anymore" story.

Did the media continue to run with it for selfish, cynical reasons? To boost their circulation and ratings? If I've learned anything after all these years as a network newsman, I know this much: never—*never!*—underestimate how low news executives, and TV people in general, will go in the pursuit of higher ratings. If CBS, ABC, and NBC News could frighten Main Street America about how AIDS was heading toward their peaceful, suburban streets *and then do stories about how scared America was*, they would do it!

But, as usual, it wasn't just ratings.

More than ever, journalists on the Left define themselves by their compassion. They might as well wear big red buttons on their lapels that say "We Care." AIDS gave them a great opportunity to care, to show how compassionate they could be. To these journalists, AIDS couldn't just be *their* disease—it had to be *everyone's* disease. Gay men along with blacks and Hispanics might be segregated from other parts of society, but when it comes to AIDS, we're all in it together. It was journalism by sentiment. As with the homeless story, this one also was being reported by the Victims of America correspondents, the ones who specialize in uncritical stories about the downtrodden.

They could unite us all. *By God, they could integrate America!* As long as they told us that AIDS was "now everybody's disease," that "now no one is safe from AIDS," then all of us—whites, blacks, Hispanics, men, women, gays, and straights—would be equals. All of us would be equally susceptible to the killer virus that, as we were so often told, "does not discriminate."

It's a good thing they were wrong. Or else we might all be dead by now. The fact is, as Michael Fumento put it in his meticulously documented 1990 book, *The Myth of Heterosexual AIDS*, "AIDS remains a disease limited primarily to specific groups engaging in specific practices."

Very politically incorrect. Fumento was actually saying that AIDS was *not* everybody's disease and that it *did* discriminate.

Heterosexuals, Fumento wrote, certainly do get AIDS. That's not the myth. But they get it "from shared needles, from transfusions, from clotting factor, which hemophiliacs use to control internal bleeding, from their mothers at or before birth, and sometimes through sexual intercourse with persons in these categories and bisexuals. The primary myth, however, was that the disease was no longer anchored to these groups but was, in fact, going from heterosexual to heterosexual to heterosexual through intercourse, that it was epidemic among non-drug-abusing heterosexuals."

Fumento had been an AIDS analyst at the U.S. Commission on Civil Rights in the Reagan administration. I interviewed him in California after his book came out, and just after he accidentally drove his brand-new sports car over a cliff on the Pacific Coast Highway. His fiancée, who was in the car with him, was hospitalized, but to the dismay of his critics, Fumento survived and, except for a few cuts, was in pretty good shape when we talked. He was friendly and certainly didn't come off as some right-wing, antigay crusader. Nonetheless, gay activists despised him because of his book. One gay journalist called him a "hate-filled, untalented lying loser." The title of Fumento's book was enough to scare many major bookstores from even carrying it, fearing picketing and worse from militant gay activists.

Some bookstore owners, those noble creatures who tell us how they would gladly die in defense of free speech, no matter how unpopular, refused to put *The Myth of Heterosexual AIDS* on their shelves. Fumento says when a friend tried to buy the book in New York City, the store manager said he didn't carry it "for editorial reasons." A doctor in San Diego, who couldn't get the book either, reported to Fumento that a store clerk told him the book was "politically incorrect."

The same high-minded philosopher/capitalists who set aside entire sections for volumes on such weighty topics as UFOs, ESP, and angels had no room for *The Myth of Heterosexual AIDS*. Fumento believes that "the AIDS crisis and the way our government, our leaders, and the media have manipulated it have provided perhaps the single best example of the politically correct intellectual dark ages into which our country has fallen."

"At least since 1986," Fumento writes, "the government has been misleading the public on the extent of the AIDS epidemic. That was when the federal Centers for Disease Control decided to move all AIDS sufferers of African and Haitian origin into the category of heterosexual AIDS cases. A man from Zaire who had sex with a dozen other men, shared needles, and had a blood transfusion would, upon diagnosis, automatically be put into the heterosexual category because of his origin.

"The result of shifting all these cases into the heterosexual category," Fumento concluded, "was a doubling of that category from 2 to 4 percent of the total. Rather than cry foul, however, our media watchdogs jumped on this statistical artifact to launch their first wave of AIDS terror."

The stories were scaring the hell out of millions of Americans. In the beginning, it probably couldn't be helped. Maybe AIDS really would start to spread among heterosexuals, through sex, from one to another to another and on and on. In the early days, I interviewed "experts" who told me exactly that—and I put it on the air.

Who knew?

But after the virus was around for a while, I started to wonder: where are all these straight Americans with AIDS? I didn't know any. My friends and neighbors didn't know any. I had read about two brothers with hemophilia who lived in my area and who died of AIDS because the clotting factor they used to control bleeding was infected with HIV. But where was this *epidemic* I kept reading about in the newspapers and hearing about on the television news?

There was no escaping the fact that the news I was getting from the press and TV didn't jibe with reality. When I read a study from the Center for Media and Public Affairs (the same research team in Washington, D.C., that had written about the real homeless versus the homeless portrayed on television), I understood why.

The center monitored network TV stories in 1992 and concluded that "TV's visual portrait of AIDS victims has little in common with real life." The center compared the people on TV, using only the information provided in the story, with "real-world data on AIDS victims compiled by the Centers for Disease Control":

■ During the period studied, 6 percent of the people with AIDS shown on the evening news were gay men. But in real life 58 percent were gay men.

■ On TV, 16 percent were blacks and Hispanics. But in real life 46 percent were black or Hispanic.

■ On TV, 2 percent of the AIDS sufferers were IV drug users. In real life 23 percent were.

"Thus, the risk groups the news audience sees are very different from their real-world counterparts," was the report's conclusion.

As with the homeless, television was back in the business of prettifying reality. Make the victims look more like you and me, and maybe we can drum up some support for their cause while we're drumming up some support for our ratings. And unlike other ailments, like cancer and heart disease, AIDS had civil rights. "How did you get it?" was considered an uncivil question.

In 1991, when Magic Johnson told the world he had HIV, Dan Rather looked into the camera and proved once again that it was more important to be politically correct than factually correct.

"As correspondent Richard Threlkeld reports, the perception may finally be catching up with the reality. That reality is: AIDS is not, quote, 'just a gay disease!'"

Then Threlkeld, a smart, veteran newsman, narrated, over pictures of Magic: "Magic Johnson's just the man to educate the rest of us about AIDS. He's not a drug user. Neither are most AIDS victims. He's heterosexual. So are four out of ten AIDS victims these days."

Let's set aside some important assumptions Threlkeld casually makes about how Magic did or did not get the virus. Because the fact is, Richard Threlkeld knows nothing about how Magic Johnson got HIV.

When Threlkeld came on the air that night and reported that four out of ten people with AIDS are heterosexuals, I got a certain impression. My guess is so did most of the people who watched the *CBS Evening News* that night.

When a reporter tells you that four out of ten people with AIDS are heterosexuals, it's reasonable to think he's talking about straight, non-IV-drug-using Americans who are getting AIDS through sexual intercourse.

But that's not at all what Richard Threlkeld was talking about.

Because most of that 40 percent Threlkeld cites got the virus *not simply because they were heterosexual* but because they were shooting up or having unprotected sex with people who were shooting up. The other heterosexuals apparently were patients in hospitals who got transfusions tainted with HIV, hemophiliacs, maybe even "heterosexual" babies born to mothers who were HIV positive. You would have to include all those groups in order to say four out of ten HIV cases involve heterosexuals.

But what if 40 percent of the people with HIV are Protestants? Or 40 percent have brown eyes? Or 40 percent have dark hair and are under six foot two? No reporter in his right mind would tell his audience, "He's Protestant and so are four out of ten victims these days." Or, "He has brown eyes and so have four out of ten victims these days."

Harry Stein, a good friend and author of *How I Accidentally Joined the Vast Right-Wing Conspiracy (and Found Inner Peace)*, wrote in his *TV Guide* column in 1994 that "AIDS is presented not just as a hideous disease, but as a gauge of our collective humanity." That is precisely why so many reporters would not ask, "How did you get it?" It somehow seemed inhumane. It seemed as if we were not sympathetic.

So when Dave Marash did his Magic Johnson story for *Nightline* on ABC, he said, "Our curiosity about people with AIDS has often been limited to one hostile question: How did you get it?"

Why in the world is that a *hostile* question? If Dave Marash did a story about lung cancer, he certainly wouldn't consider it "hostile" to ask, "How did you get it?"—especially if he knew the answer was "Three packs of Marlboros a day for twenty-five years, Dave." Dave, and every other reporter, would relish the opportunity to take on Big Tobacco, given the misery smoking has caused.

But AIDS is different. It's off limits. Only AIDS is shrouded in political correctness. We might offend gays if we ask, "How did you get it?" We fear we may look uncaring and without compassion if we ask, "How did you get it?"

In 1996, Jacqueline Adams did a story for CBS News about teenagers with AIDS and reported that the problem was mainly the result of these kids' having unprotected sex.

"Ten years ago, at age fourteen, Luna [Ortiz] was infected with the HIV virus, the very first time he had sex—unprotected sex," Adams reported.

Then she introduced us to a woman named Patricia Fleming, an AIDS activist, who said, "At least one American teenager is becoming infected every hour of every day." (Six months later, in September of 1996, another CBS News reporter, Diana Olick, reported, "The number of HIV-infected teens continues to rise. Every hour *two* kids under the age of twenty are infected." *Two—not one!* As with the homeless story, the numbers keep going higher and higher until they bear no relationship whatsoever to reality. Stay tuned!)

There was one word missing from Jacqueline Adams's story. Never, not even once, did she or any of the people she interviewed ever utter the word "gay" or "homosexual." This is quite remarkable: a story about AIDS and unprotected sex, yet the reporter doesn't tell us anything about the sexual orientation of the person with HIV.

The closest anyone came was when Luna said, "I wasn't educated about it [AIDS]. The only thing I knew was Rock Hudson died a year before." Was that the clue that Luna was gay? I don't know. Adams never told us.

By leaving out the crucial fact that almost all of these teenage AIDS cases involve homosexual sex or IV drugs or tainted blood, we are left with the impression that straight, middle-class heterosexual teens are being infected with HIV "every hour of every day."

It's simply not happening! That anyone is still contracting HIV is a tragedy of huge proportions. That the gay lobby would try to mislead us is understandable. That the media go along is disgraceful.

By now, we all know that AIDS has ravaged vast regions in Africa and that HIV is spreading like the plague through the old Soviet Union and parts of the Far East. By 2021, according to the United Nations, more than 150 million people will have been infected with HIV worldwide. By any standard, this is horrific.

We also know that in places like Africa and Russia, it isn't just gays and junkies who are contracting HIV. But by now, there's something else we know: that America is not Africa, and it's not Russia or China. We have better education about HIV here. We have better health care. Fewer people walk around with open sores on their genitals, which facilitate the transmission of the AIDS virus. Hospitals don't routinely use the same needles on many different patients. Prostitution isn't rampant the way it is in some other parts of the world. To suggest that, because AIDS is ravaging heterosexuals in parts of Uganda and China, Seattle and Kansas City are next simply is not so.

Of course, there are some places in the United States where people are so poor and where access to health care is so limited that the HIV epidemic "more closely resembles the situation of the developing world than of the rest of the country," as the *New York Times* put it on July 3, 2001.

Under a headline that read "Epidemic Takes Toll on Black Women," the *Times* told us about poor, rural southern women who were contracting HIV through unprotected heterosexual sex. For most straight Americans this is very scary news—Americans getting the AIDS virus through heterosexual intercourse! Except that, despite the headline, this wasn't simply a story about AIDS and poor black women. It was a story, as we learn in paragraph thirty-six on page twelve, about how, "As everywhere, some poor women here make ends meet through prostitution." And about how, as we're told in paragraph forty-one, "Sex is also sometimes exchanged for drugs, particularly crack cocaine."

We also learn that a majority of the women who attend one particular clinic in Greenwood, Mississippi, have a history of sexually transmitted diseases.

What all of this, taken together, means is that black women who are contracting HIV in the rural South, by and large, are not getting it simply because they are poor and black and having sex with men. They're getting it because they are engaging in high-risk sex, including having intercourse with men who use crack cocaine and probably, given the behavior of people who use crack, are also taking other drugs that involve contaminated needles.

The *Times* story was legitimate, well reported, and, I'm sure, accurate, but it was informative not just for what was in the piece but for what was left out.

Nowhere, for example, does the story actually tell us that there is no evidence that these women who contracted HIV from heterosexual men are passing the virus on to other men who are then passing it on to other women. If the virus were spreading that way—from heterosexual to heterosexual to heterosexual—it would truly be devastating information. Because then there would be proof, for the first time, that HIV really was breaking out into the low-risk general population, a deadly scenario the gay activists and the media had been warning straight America about for years.

In fact, the absence of such man-to-woman-to-man-to-woman transmission was exceedingly good news. Even in a part of America where economic and health conditions rival those in Africa, there was no evidence that the AIDS virus was ping-ponging through the heterosexual population.

But this wasn't news the *Times* thought important enough to put in this particular story. Maybe because this isn't the type of news that AIDS activists have ever wanted to get out. But the *Times* does tell us, in a small subheadline accompanying the story, "In the South, a

Different Face." But is the face really different? Yes, it's true that the face was not that of a gay white man. Or of hookers in big-city alleys shooting up heroin. Still, in the poor, rural South, like everyplace else in America, the face of AIDS is attached to people who, by and large, engage in risky sexual business—and to their newborn babies.

It's a sad story. But sometimes I get the impression that the media that have helped spread the epidemic of fear would love to spread it just a little more. Sometimes I get the impression that they'd like to write a headline that shouts: "AIDS Epidemic Takes Toll on the Middle Class." Then it really would be everyone's disease. Not just the disease of junkies and gays and poor black people in the rural South. Then no one would be safe, just as the media have been telling us for so many years. And then, finally, we would all be equal.

Here's what we do know about AIDS and HIV in America.

By the end of 1999, according to the Centers for Disease Control and Prevention (CDC), 751,965 people, living and dead, had contracted AIDS in the United States since the beginning of the epidemic:

- About 50 percent were men who had sex with other men.
- 28 percent were IV drug users.
- 6 percent more were men who had sex with men *and* injected drugs.
- 1 percent got HIV through a blood transfusion.
- Less than 1 percent were hemophiliacs.

That leaves about 13 or 14 percent—99,483 cases—listed officially as "heterosexual contact." But not just any heterosexual contact.

Of those, about 35,000 got AIDS after having sex with an IV drug user, most of them women who got HIV from a man who injected drugs. Another 4,000 women got HIV and eventually AIDS from a bisexual male. Another 1,681 got AIDS after having sex with a hemophiliac or with someone who had had a blood transfusion that was infected with HIV.

And then there's the mystery group, the group that helps feed the myth about heterosexual AIDS.

The CDC lists 58,571 people in the United States as having gotten AIDS after "sex with HIV-infected person, risk not specified."

Risk not specified! It even sounds frightening.

Does that mean that 58,000 people—about 7 percent of all the AIDS cases ever diagnosed in the United States—got AIDS simply by having sex with another heterosexual who was not in one of the high-risk groups? Is this what some scientists, public health officials, the gay special interest groups, and the media were all talking about for all these years: heterosexuals who got AIDS from other non-drug-using heterosexuals through straight sex and then passed it on to other heterosexuals who passed it on to other heterosexuals who passed it on . . . ?

Not likely. People lie about sex and sexually transmitted diseases all the time. "How did you get syphilis?" the doctor asks. "From the toilet seat," the embarrassed man or woman answers. Or simply, "I don't know." Isn't the same likely with AIDS?

The answer seems to be a strong "yes." During the mid-1980s, a New York City health department employee, Anastasia Lekatsas, who was dubbed "America's most dogged street detective of AIDS," spent hundreds of hours trying to track down the source of HIV among people who claimed they got it from heterosexual sex with someone not in a high-risk group. According to the *New York Times*, "If a man claimed to have gotten AIDS from a woman, she would visit him, revisit him, interview his family and friends—and eventually she would almost always find that he'd been sharing needles or having sex with men."

So how many heterosexual Americans got AIDS from another heterosexual *not in a high-risk group?* Nobody knows. But the data would indicate the number is very, very small.

Whatever it is, it's too high. Too tragic. But it simply doesn't warrant the panic the media put America through. When the cover of *Life* told us in 1985 that "Now No One Is Safe from AIDS," it had the story all wrong. So did all the others that warned of the coming heterosexual AIDS epidemic.

Maybe not in the beginning, but at some point, reporters should have known better. Still, they continued to spread the myth of heterosexual AIDS, letting their compassion get in the way of their reporting, just as they did with the homeless story. Reporters were again doing the work of the activists because they sympathized with the cause. While it might have seemed compassionate, in a liberal kind of way, it might have had the opposite effect of what they intended.

"The first step in controlling a communicable disease," Michael Fumento wrote, "is to determine who is getting it and how. The disinformation campaign that grossly overemphasized the groups and activities least at risk of getting AIDS does those in greater jeopardy no favor."

There's another way to look at it. What is it costing the media to be generous—to suspend our healthy journalistic skepticism—when people are in real need? By spreading fear about AIDS—by doing the work of gay activists—we journalists got Washington to pay attention, didn't we? There's so much to gain by being compassionate. The only thing we lose is our credibility.

"The Killer Next Door" is what the prime-time CBS News program *48 Hours* called its show about AIDS in the suburbs. Great title. Especially if you're trying to scare the hell out of your audience and get good ratings at the same time.

"The Killer Next Door" was shot in 1992, mostly in Orange County, California—home of John Wayne Airport and for a long time the very symbol of conservative, middle-class, white, suburban America. That, of course, was the point—that AIDS was now everyone's disease, that it was no longer just the disease of gay men in places like Greenwich

Village and the Castro section of San Francisco—or mostly black and Hispanic junkies in Harlem and Watts. AIDS was now "The Killer Next Door."

It was a dramatic and scary program . . . and monumentally dishonest.

"Kimberly Richards has AIDS," reporter Erin Moriarty tells us. "She is twenty-five years old."

Kimberly lets us know that "I'm middle class, I'm college educated, I'm married, and I have a baby. That's not what doctors think a person with HIV is."

Moriarty reports that "Kimberly thinks she was infected through unprotected sex when she was a teenager." She lets it go at that, leaving us to believe that not only was Kimberly your typical American suburban teenager, but so was the boy she had sex with. You see how easy it is for any of us to get AIDS? My God, it really is "The Killer Next Door."

But wouldn't we have learned more if we had known whether Kimberly was having unprotected sex with an IV drug user? Did she ever inject herself with a needle to shoot drugs? Moriarty doesn't go into that, either. All we need to know is that Kimberly is white, suburban, and college educated—just like many of the people sitting at home watching *48 Hours*, and their kids. If Kimberly can get AIDS. . . .

Then reporter Richard Schlesinger takes us to Orange County's Foothill High School and tells us that it's a place "where, like so many other places in suburban America, children are waking to a frightening new fact of life: the shadow of certain death."

Children waking to a new reality—the shadow of certain death? This is what happens when entertainment "values" infect the news. We get writing that sounds more like a promotional blurb for a Stephen King thriller than nonfiction copy for a program produced by CBS News.

Schlesinger goes on to describe an assembly at Foothill High, where the three guest speakers all have the AIDS virus. One of them, Schlesinger reports, is special, in that her "words strike particularly close to home." Why? Because, she tells the assembly, while the *48 Hours* cameras are rolling, "I graduated from Foothill in 1984. . . . I was sitting where you were, you know. Please don't be sitting where I am a few years from now."

It's terribly sad. So sad that Richard Schlesinger doesn't think we need to know anything more. How she got the virus is something Schlesinger doesn't get into. Was she shooting up? Who knows? No hostile questions allowed.

The other speakers tell their stories, too. One of them, a man, says, "The AIDS virus can attack any race, social class, sex, or age group."

True enough. Straight, middle-class suburbanites could get AIDS and so could teenagers in small-town America. There were well-publicized and very sad stories in the fall of 1997 about the girls in Jamestown, New York, who befriended a New York City junkie. He had made frequent trips upstate, won the girls over, had sex with them, and left them with HIV. But by and large, heterosexuals who didn't befriend drug addicts had a greater chance of drowning in a bathtub than getting AIDS.

But the aim, of course, of this young man with the AIDS virus at Foothill High in Orange County, California, was to scare the hell out of the kids in front of him. And *48 Hours*'s point was to scare the hell out of America. Scaring the hell out of people makes for good television even when it makes for shallow journalism. So *48 Hours* believes we don't need to know any of the details about this person with HIV, either.

On and on it goes in white, suburban, middle-class Orange Country throughout the *48 Hours* program. Only one young man with HIV says he's gay. The others either tell *48 Hours* they don't know how they got the virus or they don't say even that much. And, of course, *48 Hours* doesn't ask. Because the wrong answers could ruin the premise of the whole show. AIDS, after all, is "The Killer Next Door."

Andrew Heyward was then the executive producer of *48 Hours*. I told him I thought he put the show on for just one reason: ratings.

He was annoyed and said something like, "I can't believe you think I would do that."

Of course I think he would do that.

In the old days, hour-long CBS News programs, like *CBS Reports*, tackled the big issues of our times, and producers were not expected to get big ratings. The men who started up the networks in the earliest days of television thought news was special. They made their money on Lucy and Ricky and Jackie Gleason and Jack Benny. For years and years, news wasn't a money-maker and wasn't expected to be.

Don Hewitt, the creator and executive producer of *60 Minutes*, loves to tell the story about how, when the show first went on the air, Bill Paley, the founder of CBS, told him, "Make us proud!"

"Now," Hewitt says, "they tell us: Make us money!"

It's ironic that *60 Minutes*, far and away the best of all the news magazine shows, indirectly is responsible for the "infotainment" we see on prime-time magazine programs today. *60 Minutes* started out to do good—and it also did quite well. It made the network a not-so-small fortune over the years. When the corporate executives realized news could actually make money, all bets were off.

In the 1970s, Dick Salant, perhaps the most revered president in all of CBS News's long history, came back to the Broadcast Center from a meeting across town at Black Rock, the CBS corporate headquarters in Manhattan, and told his top staff, "I have good news and bad news; what do you want to hear first?"

"Give us the good news first," someone said.

"The good news is that CBS News last quarter [thanks to *60 Minutes*] made money for the first time ever."

"What's the bad news?" someone else asked.

"The bad news is that CBS News made money for the first time ever."

Salant knew. They all knew. If news could actually make money, the suits who ran the network would expect just that. Sure they would want quality, in theory. But they wanted ratings and money, in fact.

It took a while but along came *20/20* and *48 Hours* and *Dateline* and a million others that didn't last. Whatever else they did, they were expected to turn a profit. When they did, they were cloned, like *Rocky* movies. There was *Dateline II* and *III* and *IV* and whatever it's up to now. There were *20/20* clones. Even *60 Minutes* got cloned.

So if Andrew Heyward didn't get ratings for *48 Hours* and didn't make the network money, they'd cancel it. He knew it, and he lived with that sword hanging over his head every single week. When the geniuses at CBS in Hollywood were about to cancel *48 Hours* in its infancy in the early 1990s, Heyward convinced them to give the show a new time slot. "If we don't survive in the new slot," he told them, "cancel us."

The deal with the devil had been struck. The first week in the new time slot, Heyward broadcast "Spring Break," one of the most humiliating shows *48 Hours* has ever put on the air. There was no point to it, except to show beautiful coeds in skimpy bikinis hanging out on the beach in Fort Lauderdale. There was a lot of chitchat about sex and beer and that, pretty much, was that.

"Spring Break" got one of the highest ratings in the entire history of *48 Hours*. Eric Ober, then the president of CBS News, threw the staff an ice cream and cake party.

Case closed!

So, do I believe my good friend Andrew Heyward would put on a scary program whose primary goal was to get high ratings even if it meant telling half-truths about who was getting AIDS in America and how they were getting it?

In a word, *Yes!*

To make matters worse, Heyward let a gay man who was dying of AIDS produce "The Killer Next Door." I'm not saying he wasn't capable of being objective, just that he wasn't.

"If you want to give Rob a going-away present," I told Heyward, "you ought to do it on your own time."

I knew it sounded cold, but I believed it was true. Heyward wanted blond-haired, blue-eyed people with HIV on his program for his own reasons—ratings! This particular producer was more than willing to deliver, for his own reasons. He wanted to scare America into believing that AIDS really was menacing white, suburban, middle-class communities; to enlist white, suburban, middle-class Americans in a war to wake up the Republican politicians in Washington, whom the AIDS lobby blamed for doing nothing to wipe out the disease.

I told Heyward that given the overwhelming slant to the program, I wanted to do a story for the show that explored the other side, the side that questioned whether AIDS really was "The Killer Next Door." I told him I wanted to interview several people, including Randy Shilts, the best-informed journalist on AIDS in all of America.

Heyward said okay. So I flew off to San Francisco to meet Shilts, who had written the brilliant book *And the Band Played On*, a devastating history of neglect on the part of our government and the medical establishment in the early years of the AIDS epidemic. Randy Shilts was gay himself.

Shilts and I spoke in a beautiful park overlooking San Francisco. People were throwing Frisbees and sunbathing, and we were talking about the virus that was ravaging his city—and how the media were handling it.

"Why did so many reporters run with the heterosexual AIDS story?" I asked him.

"This was a new angle on the story," he said, "and we need something that brings the story home to most of our readers. Most of our readers or viewers are going to be heterosexuals. I think that there were some crasser considerations. If you want to sell newspapers or get people to watch your show, you want to say, 'This is a threat to you, too.'"

Shilts knew the real story and he wasn't afraid to tell it. We walked through gay neighborhoods in San Francisco, and he pointed to houses where friends had lived and died. He cared deeply about all of them. But he didn't let his compassion stand in the way of his journalism.

Randy Shilts knew that AIDS was not really "The Killer Next Door," not the way we were playing it, anyway. It was "The Killer Next Door" in his neighborhood—but not in all of our neighborhoods.

"A lot of heterosexuals are looking down their cul-de-sacs and seeing that the Grim Reaper is not walking down their tree-lined streets," he told me. "There was a profound frustration among AIDS activists and among AIDS researchers that the only time the media seemed to pay attention to AIDS, the only time the government seemed to do anything about AIDS, was when it appeared that it would affect heterosexuals."

So the activists did what they felt they had to do. They got the word out that it would spread to all of us. And the media passed it along to America, at first because they didn't know better, then because they thought heterosexual AIDS was a better story, but eventually because it was another way to show compassion.

So we showed people with AIDS on television and never bothered to say they were gay. We showed straight suburbanites with AIDS and never bothered to ask if they shot drugs into their veins or had sex with people who did.

Even before "The Killer Next Door" aired, there was a buzz around the *48 Hours* shop about the story I had covered. The producer I worked with, Liza McGuirk, who is one of the best in the business, told me that some of our colleagues were not at all happy. While everyone else was going along with the program, reporting about AIDS in middle-class, heterosexual America, Liza and I were saying "not so fast," the Grim Reaper was *not* walking down those tree-lined suburban streets.

"How could you have done that?" a *48 Hours* staffer asked Liza in that annoying, whiny tone that suggests that you—*someone as decent and sensitive as you, Liza!*—should know better. They were disappointed that Liza McGuirk, who was well liked and respected, would take part in a story that didn't toe the party line on AIDS. Some of the producers who were gay were downright angry—and they let Liza know it. For whatever reason, they didn't confront me directly, which was probably a good idea all the way around.

Randy Shilts died one year and ten months after I interviewed him on that clear, crisp, beautiful day in San Francisco. He died of AIDS, just like so many of his friends before him. Randy Shilts didn't tell any of us that he had the disease when we spoke. Yet he was brave enough to tell the truth. He was courageous enough to say that despite what the media were telling America, AIDS was not "The Killer Next Door." Not the way we were suggesting, anyway.

If Randy Shilts could be that honest, why can't the rest of us?

"I Thought Our Job Was to Tell the Truth" **7**

In 1995, the state of Alabama decided to go back to the future. Apparently, they had a failure to communicate down there. Some prison inmates weren't following the rules, so the people in charge decided to make clear what exactly the relationship was between crime and punishment in the great state of Alabama.

Which is why they resurrected the old chain gang.

Before Alabama decided to send a message to its criminals, the only place you could find a chain gang was in the classic movie section at Blockbuster. In real life, chain gangs had been abolished a long time ago. Taking prisoners in chains out in the fields, putting them under the hot sun, and making them work while guards with shotguns kept a close eye on them in some circles was considered a throwback to a less enlightened time in America.

Which is exactly what made it such a good story. It's also what sent the politically correct, sensitive, liberal producers who ran the *CBS Evening News* with Dan Rather into a New York City tizzy.

The evening news sent Larry Doyle, who was based in Miami, to Alabama to produce the story. Doyle is an ex-marine captain who jumped out of helicopters in Vietnam. He's a tough, no-nonsense guy who thinks Marlboros and Heineken are two of the essential food groups. And he's one of the best hard news producers at CBS or any of the networks.

Doyle hooked up with a CBS News reporter named Diana Gonzalez and together they flew off to Alabama. There was an old joke at the time about how pilots would come on the PA system as the plane left Florida airspace and tell the passengers, "We've just crossed into Alabama; set your watches back—one hundred years." It was cheap but not completely unfounded.

From the airport in Montgomery, they drove to a farm in rural Alabama, where the prison officials were waiting for their arrival. Over the years, certainly during the dark, nasty days of the civil rights marches, reporters from places like CBS News were about as welcome in Alabama as a black woman determined to sit in the front of the bus.

But not today. Today the people who ran the farm were glad to see Doyle and Gonzalez. They were proud of their chain gang and didn't care one bit if the whole world knew about it. So they gave the CBS camera crew the green light to shoot a chain gang, which was made up of twenty convicts, shackled at the ankles in groups of five, doing various chores on the farm. (In Alabama, the chain gang wasn't for everybody, just special cases—repeat offenders and troublemakers.)

Doyle remembers it was a typical summer afternoon in Alabama—real hot and real humid. You could see the heat waves coming off the country roads, he told me. The convicts, who were breaking rocks and tilling soil and doing other odd jobs around the farm, predictably were not happy.

"This makes you hate," one of them told Diana, while looking straight at the CBS News camera.

"I ain't no damn dog, not me. I'm a man," another told her.

"It makes you feel like a slave," said a third.

Doyle and Gonzalez also got an interview with the biggest backer of the chain gang in the entire state of Alabama, Governor Fob James.

"In Alabama, if you break the law, and if you assault people, hurt people, rape and rob, you're gonna wind up in the chain gang," is how the governor put it. And then, as if we didn't know, he added, "I like that."

TV producers are the equivalent of newspaper editors, so Doyle matched Diana Gonzalez's script with pictures of the chain gang, supervised the videotape editing of the story, and then sent it via satellite to New York. It aired on the evening news. And that, Doyle figured, was that.

Until the next day, when he got a call from Al Berman, one of the senior producers on the *CBS Evening News*. It seems that Doyle hadn't bothered to "warn" the senior producers that all but one of the men in the chain gang were black.

It wasn't an issue as far as Doyle was concerned. He covered the story that was there, edited it, and sent the videotape to New York. The first time the *CBS Evening News* senior producers realized the chain gang was almost all black was when they watched the story come off the satellite. It was right before airtime and by then it was too late to do anything but put the story on television.

"Was that a representative sample of the prisoners?" Berman wanted to know.

"Yes, it was," Doyle said.

"Was it a fair portrayal of who the prisoners were?" Berman went on.

"Yeah."

"Well, we have to be more careful next time," Doyle recalls Berman telling him. "We don't want to give the impression that the only prisoners down there are black.

One of the things I like best about Larry Doyle is that he has virtually no tolerance for bullshit. He's a tough guy, in the Hemingway mold, who could tell great stories about hot spots he's covered all over the world. He is intelligent and funny and always a straight shooter. You know where you stand with Larry Doyle. And Al Berman was about to find out where *he* stood with Larry Doyle. This conversation on the phone was setting off Doyle's bullshit detector.

Doyle was getting annoyed as he listened to this lecture, coming from one of the New York producers, a group (at least as far as I'm concerned) not known for its sophistication when it comes to things like life in Alabama. Or like life anyplace outside the Upper West Side of Manhattan, for that matter.

This was a group that would rather vacation on the dark side of the moon than so much as set foot in a place as unappealing and unsophisticated (*to them anyway!*) as Alabama, where they might have to come into contact with—*it was too painful to say—Alabamians!,* some of whom actually might not have attended college in the Northeast—*or anyplace else*—and where you probably couldn't even get the early edition of the *New York Times*.

"I shot what was there," Doyle told Berman, an edge creeping into his voice. Berman told Doyle to be more careful next time. To get more pictures of white criminals next time.

The conversation was idiotic as far as Larry Doyle was concerned. There was just *one* white criminal! *What was he supposed to do? This was Alabama, for crissake, not fucking Switzerland!*

The talk wasn't going anywhere; Doyle wanted to go. He had had enough of Al Berman. Doyle was no bigot, and he didn't like the implication that he was. So he ended the call with a witty and sophisticated pleasantry that Noël Coward himself would have envied.

"Fuck off," Doyle explained.

Al Berman isn't a bad guy. He was just trying to be compassionate. And since race in America is the wound that never seems to heal, sensitivity isn't a bad thing.

But what if journalistic sensitivity had led Berman and the other *CBS Evening News* senior producers down a different road?

"Are the Alabama authorities unfairly rounding up black men?" they could have asked.

"Are they convicting black men of crimes that white men don't get convicted of, maybe don't even get arrested for?" they could have asked.

"Are the authorities labeling black convicts 'troublemakers' in order to funnel them onto the chain gang—*simply because they are black?* Is that why the ratio on the chain gang was about nineteen to one?"

If any of the answers had been "yes," it would have made a great story, which also might have done some real good. But to get the facts for a story like that would be hard, time-consuming, expensive work. The *CBS Evening News* in New York didn't send Doyle to Alabama to spend money and time. He was there to get a good picture story, fast.

"Convicts in chains" is what they sent him to Alabama to get. For sound bites, he was supposed to round up the usual suspects: the governor giving the pros of the chain gang, the cons giving the cons.

Image is what the TV producers in New York were concerned about. Let's not make it look like it really is. That might cause problems. That might make us look insensitive and short on compassion.

Distort the images. If those black men in Alabama were actually being railroaded simply because of their race, let someone else, with more time and money, worry about that. Being compassionate in television news these days means never having to get your hands dirty.

Instead of manipulating the images and then convincing ourselves that we were sensitive and therefore had actually accomplished something, we should have been looking at race and sensitivity in a totally different way. If being sensitive and trying to accomplish something was the goal, we should have been expanding our Rolodex files to include more black people.

We should have put more black environmentalists in our stories, and more black scientists, and more black businessmen and women. We should have put black people in our stories to talk about a whole range of issues besides race, which is about the only thing we let black people talk about on television (except for sports). That would get black Americans on national television in a positive light, and it would be a lot more honest than simply using de facto racial quotas to make sure we put enough white criminals on the air to balance the number of black criminals we were showing.

But in the hands of journalism's ayatollahs of political correctness, even a well-intentioned goal to get more minorities in news stories, in a positive light, can get downright silly.

Brill's Content, in 1999, told a story about the Gannett newspaper chain's policy that *requires* reporters at all seventy-five Gannett papers to include minority sources in all their stories.

Jennifer Greenstein, who wrote the piece, tells about a reporter at Gannett's *Greenville News* in South Carolina who spent hours hunting for a black person to include in a story about...*Hanukkah food!* Religious minorities don't count with Gannett, so the reporter had to find someone who was both Jewish and a racial minority. Too bad Sammy Davis Jr. is dead.

"I couldn't find any Ethiopian Jews," the reporter is quoted as saying. "I called the synagogue and asked if they had any African Jews. They said no."

What a surprise. No African Jews living in Greenville, South Carolina.

The same reporter spent a good part of another day trying to find a nonwhite person to quote in a story on gourmet dog biscuits, a subject that cries out for minority expertise.

Another reporter at the same *Greenville News* estimates he "made an extra thirty phone calls" before he found an Asian astronomer in Utah for a story about a solar eclipse.

A Japanese woman who lives in Greenville was quoted three times in thirteen days, telling the paper's readers what she thought about a local jogging path ("It's inspiring to me"), about the importance of changing an area rug each season ("It's very important to respect the seasons"), and about an upcoming Elton John concert ("I think it's a good follow-up after Janet Jackson").

"Never mind," Ms. Greenstein tells us, "that [the Japanese source] isn't an Elton John fan, and doesn't have any particular expertise on jogging or area rugs. She fit the bill." Translation: she wasn't white.

"It's hard to quarrel with the goal," Ms. Greenstein points out. And she's right. A policy that gives minorities an opportunity to air their views about something other than being minorities is a pretty good idea. A little more common sense, when it comes to stories about Hanukkah food, would make it a great idea.

A few months after the chain gang incident, in September 1995, Larry Doyle was in St. Thomas, in the Virgin Islands, covering Hurricane Marilyn. Looting had become a problem, and Doyle and his camera crew were right there on a downtown street when the police rounded up some looters and hauled them off to jail.

As Yogi Berra might have put it, it was déjà vu all over again.

At CBS News in New York, weekend news producers were watching Doyle's story come in off the satellite, and one of them didn't like what she was seeing.

According to Doyle, Raylena Fields complained to the others that all the looters in Doyle's piece were black. So was she. Apparently, she didn't like the idea that CBS News would put those pictures on the air. So she let the senior producers know how she felt.

Such an expression of concern carries a lot of weight in network newsrooms. White producers are very sensitive to what black colleagues feel. Partly because white news people understand that they can't see things in quite the same way that black journalists can and partly because they don't want to be seen as racists.

Michael Janeway, the former editor in chief of the *Boston Globe*, writes about this practice—newsroom monitors keeping an eye out for stories that might offend. In his book *Republic of Denial*, Janeway says, "Suddenly newsrooms had de facto caucuses organized by gender, race, and ethnicity. Suddenly coverage of controversial stories had to be negotiated within the newsroom as well as outside."

Which is what was happening with the looting episode in Doyle's hurricane story. Fields had made her case in New York, and now her concerns were being passed on to Doyle in the Virgin Islands.

He didn't like the implication one bit, that maybe the looting shots didn't bother him because he wasn't as sensitive as they thought he should be—or worse, that he was some kind of bigot.

"It's not every day you're accused of being a racist," he told me years later.

"Yes," he told the New York producers by phone, "the looters *are* black. And so are the *cops* who arrested them. *And so is 95 percent of the island!*"

Fields doesn't dispute the basic facts, but she told me that what bothered her about the pictures was the implication that the looting was widespread, that it was happening all over the island in the aftermath of the storm. In fact, she said, looting was "minor" and "very limited." The pictures, in her view, placed high up in the story, and the words that went along with them, were misleading, and that's why she objected.

It's a seductive argument. But what if the hurricane had blown through Naples, Florida, instead of the Virgin Islands, and the "minor" and "very limited" looting was the work of young *white* men? Would Raylena Fields and the other producers in New York have shown the same concern about the impression those pictures might leave? After all, it wasn't widespread—and most young white men in Naples aren't looters.

Most white businessmen aren't criminals, either, but TV producers don't hesitate to show the few who are being led off in handcuffs for allegedly manipulating the stock market. Most deadbeat dads aren't rich doctors, but we put them on the air every chance we get if they're being marched off to jail for failing to pay child support.

It's called news. And so is looting after a hurricane. Even if it is "minor" and "very limited," and, yes, even if the looters are black.

I understand that in this country there is an ugly history that involves race, which is different from anything else in our past. I understand that putting white businessmen and rich doctors on TV in a bad light doesn't reflect on all white businessmen or all rich doctors. But putting black looters on TV doesn't reflect on all black people, either. The only people who think it does are either stupid or racist. I don't think we should be making news decisions based on those two groups of losers. It's true that once in our not-too-distant past, journalists, like many Americans, weren't sensitive enough about race, and we came away with nasty stereotypes about black people. But the pendulum has taken a long, long swing over the years. Now we have debates and seminars in the newsroom about whether it's proper to show black police arresting a few black looters in a predominantly black country.

The hurricane story ran, but Raylena Fields had prevailed on her sensitive colleagues, who took out the looting shot. Journalistically, this was questionable, at best. But journalism wasn't the only issue on the table. Satisfying a black colleague—and rectifying three hundred or four hundred years of American Racial Sin—was also a consideration.

"I thought our job was to tell the truth," Doyle told me.

Apparently, it's not that simple, because reporters and producers in the field got the same song and dance from the Sensitivity Patrol in New York over and over again.

Andy Triay, a producer in the Miami bureau of CBS News, was covering a story about two white men who were accused of abducting a black man near Tampa, Florida, and forcing him at gunpoint to drive to a remote field, where they doused him with gasoline and set him on fire.

In the script, which Triay e-mailed to his bosses at the *CBS Evening News*, the victim was described as "a black man." A senior producer told Triay to change the description from "black" to "African-American," the term considered more progressive in some circles.

This may seem harmless enough . . . except for one thing. "The victim isn't American," Triay told the producer. "He's from Jamaica, in the Caribbean."

That, one might reasonably conclude, would have been the end of the matter. But it wasn't. "Change it to African-American or the story doesn't get on the air," she told Triay.

He made the change, knowing it was wrong, and later Andy told me, "Everyone involved in that matter knew that if we called him African-American we would be factually incorrect. But to get the story on the air, we had to do it."

Maybe it was no big deal. The world didn't come to an end. Nor did it come to an end when producers in New York complained, as they often did, that prison stories showed too many black inmates and not enough white ones. Even though in some parts of the country, especially in the South, the prison population is heavily black.

Being sensitive is not a bad thing, and being concerned about how people are portrayed is no small matter, either. But this sensitivity, it seems to me, stems from something deeper and more complicated than plain old-fashioned decency.

The liberal media elites are not some alien species. They're part of the bigger liberal community—a community, according to the brilliant author and scholar Shelby Steele, that has been on a journey for some time now, a journey to redemption from racial guilt.

"I think that white guilt, in its broad sense, springs from a *knowledge* of ill-gotten advantage," Steele, who is black, writes in *The Content of*

Our Character, his powerful book about race in America. "More precisely, it comes from the juxtaposition of this knowledge with the inevitable gratitude one feels for being white rather than black in America."

This same guilt, maybe also *this gratitude for being white rather than black in America*, I believe, is what drives many white media elites to obsess about such things as the number of blacks we show on the chain gang. Or to make sure we don't call a black man from the Caribbean "black" but "African-American," because somehow we think that title bestows more respect. Or to shy away from showing black looters on an island populated overwhelmingly by black people.

This business of playing with the images and being ultrasensitive to what we label people is not about *actually* doing good. If doing good were what it was about, we'd spend lots of money investigating why so many blacks wind up on the chain gang. That might *really* accomplish something. When you get right down to it, this compassion wasn't for the downtrodden at all. It was for us. All this concern wasn't about injustices. It was about feeling better about *ourselves*—and making as little personal sacrifice as possible.

I once suggested to Andrew Heyward that there was a foolproof way to change the racial power structure in America—not in ten or twenty years, but literally overnight.

"Effective right now," I said, "you and every other white male high-level executive in America should *voluntarily* give up your jobs—on one condition: that you be replaced by a qualified woman or member of a minority group starting tomorrow morning. The face of corporate America would immediately change. Whaddaya think?"

The king was not amused. Andrew Heyward did not like the idea. Not one bit. That would have cost him something, and that's not how the game works. But making sure we call Jamaicans "African-American" instead of "black" and making sure we limit the number of black criminals we put on the TV screen cost Heyward and the other media elites nothing—and that's just how they like it.

Redemption for America's—and the media's—deplorable racial history never came so cheap.

They love affirmative action, as long as their own kids get into Ivy League schools. They love handing out jobs based on racial preferences, as long as they get to keep theirs. It's a great deal: it's always somebody else who has to make the sacrifice—sometimes Asian-American kids, sometimes other white students who don't get into places like Harvard and Yale and Princeton—while the white liberal elites get to claim credit for being so decent, the saviors of black people in America.

"What the liberal really wants is to bring about change which will not in any way endanger his position," is how Stokely Carmichael once put it.

So in the end, the liberals who command the highest positions among the media elites are not generous at all. They're quite selfish, really. They distort images *not* to ease the pain of oppressed black Americans, but to ease *their own pain*, to make themselves feel less guilty, and, most important, to prove how good and caring *they* are.

As long as there are victims in America, real or otherwise, and as long as there are self-centered, guilt-ridden reporters and editors, the Me Decade will never end.

How About a Media That Reflects America? 8

The News Mafia was all over me, and no one with any
brains was taking bets that I would survive.

Dan Rather made sure I was kept off the air (or off his
evening newscast anyway), which is death to a television
reporter. Peter Johnson, who writes a TV column in *USA Today*—and
who would break his nose on Dan's behind if the anchorman ever
stopped quickly—wrote that many of my colleagues dismissed me as
"dead wrong, an ingrate, a nut, or all of the above."

And that was the good news!

The bad news was that the anti-Christ, Rush Limbaugh, and the
other conservative elites, had come riding to my defense. I would have
been a lot better off if Saddam Hussein, O. J. Simpson, and Charles
Manson had held a joint news conference to tell the world what a great
guy I was.

Limbaugh read my *Wall Street Journal* column on his radio program,
which went out to millions of Americans who didn't trust the big-time

media long before I threw my two cents into the debate. Rush, predictably, agreed with every word. So did his callers.

At the time, Limbaugh also had a syndicated television show, and one night he devoted a long segment (six minutes and twenty-seven seconds) to what he saw as monumental hypocrisy on the part of CBS News.

This is a business, he told his audience, "that seeks whistle-blowers out; they love dirty little secrets."

Limbaugh said I was in trouble for nothing more than "calling it like it is."

"Here's a guy who says what I would venture 70 percent of the American people agree with—that the press is liberal—and he's in huge trouble."

Yes, and it got a lot huger after Limbaugh's testimonial.

"Rather is furious," Heyward told me. Whether he watched the TV show or heard the radio version or someone told him about one or the other, I don't know. It didn't matter. Limbaugh was on my side, and, as mad as Rather was before, he was a lot madder now.

Getting support from Rush Limbaugh comes with a lot of baggage. Two years earlier, Jeffrey Goodell wrote in *Elle* magazine about Limbaugh's support for another journalist, Emily Rooney (Andy's daughter), who had been pushed out the door at ABC News.

"This afternoon it's not the pressure of the job that's getting to [now-fired *World News Tonight* executive producer Emily] Rooney," Goodell wrote. "It's Rush Limbaugh. Limbaugh read from a story in *TV Guide* . . . in which Rooney gently chastises the media for its liberal vision. It's the truth, of course—media executives know it, correspondents know it, and the viewers out in TV-land know it. But for a television executive to come out and say it is a real no-no, a violation of clan rules. And to have Limbaugh on your side—what could be worse? Within the liberal orthodoxy of ABC News, being championed by Rush Limbaugh is akin to being seen huddling with a child molester."

I didn't want to become a darling of conservatives. Sure, I was a critic of the networks' leftward tilt just as they were, but I wasn't part of some right-wing cabal, no matter how many times Dan Rather implied it.

The fact is, I would have loved to get some support from the Left, from people like Frank Rich of the *New York Times*, and Jonathan Alter of *Newsweek*, and Ellen Goodman of the *Boston Globe*. But nothing I said in the *Wall Street Journal* piqued their interest in the least.

I would have been thrilled if *New York Times* columnist Anthony Lewis, who is so very sensitive to all sorts of "chilling effects," had shown just a little sensitivity to the plight of a reporter whose job was hanging by a thread because he wasn't diplomatic, because he actually had the nerve to *publicly* express an unpopular view about—oh my God!—the press.

I guess I was naive, but I thought liberals should be concerned about that kind of "chilling effect" too. But they weren't.

Liberals in the media—who would have come down with the vapors if a conservative CEO had so much as given a reporter a dirty look—didn't flinch when CBS News executives took me off the air and suggested I might be fired because they saw me as a whistle-blower, which, the best I could figure, made me the first whistle-blower in history who wasn't turned into a national hero by the media.

If I had worked at Firestone and blown the whistle on defective tires, *60 Minutes* would have immortalized me. Lesley Stahl would have portrayed me as the courageous David going up against the corporate Goliath and would have lobbied Congress to make my birthday a national holiday.

Unfortunately, the defective product I was making noise about wasn't tires; it was network news. Andrew Heyward even told me that Don Hewitt, who had put more whistle-blowers on the air than anyone in broadcasting history, said, "I don't want him [Goldberg] anywhere on the ninth floor," where *60 Minutes* is located at CBS News in New York.

One of my few remaining friends on the *CBS Evening News*, a young producer named Mitch Weitzner, who didn't approve of what I had done or how I had done it, told me that writing the op-ed "wasn't courageous. It was stupid."

"What do you think would have happened to you if you worked at IBM and did something like this?" Technically it was a question, but Mitch was really making a statement, not just about the wisdom, but about the morality of airing your own company's dirty laundry in public.

All I could say was, "But this isn't IBM. Or General Motors. They don't look down everybody's throat for a living. This is CBS News. We do. And that makes all the difference in the world."

In the midst of all this, only one important journalist who was not a member of the vast right-wing conspiracy weighed in with even indirect support. Michael Gartner, the former newspaper editor, Pulitzer Prize winner, and past president of NBC News, wrote about my situation in his *USA Today* column.

"The issue is important," Gartner wrote, "and Heyward could use it to make CBS a journalistic leader. Whatever he may think of Goldberg's broadside, he publicly should embrace his reporter, say that he's glad CBS journalists care about fairness, and declare that the controversy should raise the network's consciousness about fairness.

"CBS could lead the way. It might be painful, but people would notice. Heyward and Goldberg could change the business. And it might even unmire them from third place. . . . Taking sides isn't good journalism. Taking care is."

Andrew Heyward never said a word to me about Gartner's friendly advice. All I know is that he didn't take it.

The *New York Post*, a conservative paper, came to my defense. In an editorial headlined "Blowing the Whistle on CBS News," the *Post* said, "CBS News, which prides itself on its bold willingness to expose the dark secrets of corporate America, has apparently discovered that the truth hurts.

"CBS is working itself into a state of high dudgeon over Goldberg's decision to go public with his views," the *Post* went on. *"Evening News* anchor Dan Rather 'deplores' the whole situation. CBS News president Andrew Heyward is said to be livid. No one, however, appears ready to dispute the details in which Goldberg's analysis is grounded.

"We can sympathize with the suggestion that trust within a company is undermined when isolated individuals bare dirty linen in public. But it comes with little grace for CBS News to take refuge in this line of argument. After all, many Americans were introduced to the concept of corporate 'whistle-blowers' by CBS journalists."

And the *Post* concluded, "It's worth remembering that whistle-blowers can tell all kinds of truths. And it's just as important for the American people to understand how bias taints the news disseminated by the major networks as it is for them to grasp the alleged inner workings of tobacco companies."

Cal Thomas, the conservative syndicated columnist, wrote, "CBS News correspondent Bernard Goldberg... has blown what cover remains on the contention that the networks are fair, balanced, and unbiased.... Goldberg provided a rare glimpse from the inside. It will be interesting to see if he's allowed to keep his job now that the dirty little secret is finally out."

I was wondering the exact same thing.

At about 12:20 in the afternoon on February 21, 1996, eight days after the op-ed came out, I spoke by phone with Jon Klein, the executive vice president of CBS News and Heyward's number two in command.

"Is CBS News going to fire me?" I asked him point-blank.

"If we wanted to fire you," Klein said, "we would have fired you the day the *Wall Street Journal* piece ran."

This was the first indication that *perhaps* I might survive.

Klein, in his forties, is an Ivy Leaguer, a graduate of Brown. He's very smart, but, like a lot of TV executives, he's someone you wouldn't want to turn your back on. Jon is on the small, thin side, wears eyeglasses, and comes off as a cross between a well-dressed Woody Allen . . . and Machiavelli. He's very creative, but at CBS News he had a reputation as the kind of guy who thought people who tell the truth do it mainly because they lack imagination.

So when he hinted that I might survive, I was skeptical.

If CBS had done that—fired me the day the *WSJ* piece came out—I told Klein, it would have touched off a major battle CBS News didn't need.

"Can you imagine the headlines?" I said. "'The House That Murrow Built Fires Correspondent for Taking on Bias in the News.'" I was talking with far more confidence than I actually had. "CBS News Unloads Renegade Correspondent," was more like it.

"If CBS News had fired me the day the op-ed piece came out," I told Klein, "it would have been a public relations disaster." After all, millions of Americans agree with me, I told him. Once you leave Manhattan, you hear all the time about how biased the big, national media are.

I was whistling past the graveyard.

Klein was calm and matter-of-fact. I've never known him to get rattled. So he first reminded me that by writing the op-ed piece I had violated my contract, which says that CBS News journalists had to get prior approval before submitting articles for publication. Technically, CBS News could have fired me for that and that alone, he said, and technically I guess he was right. But I reminded him that others, including Dan Rather, had written controversial op-ed pieces without getting approval, and nothing ever happened to any of them.

Good point, I thought, but I knew it wasn't good enough to save me if that's what it came down to.

I also knew that the United States Constitution wasn't going to save me, either. I understood that I had no First Amendment, free-speech rights. The First Amendment prohibits only *government* from telling us what we can and can't say. Corporations are not democracies. Nor should they be. They're more like dictatorships, when you get right down to it—some run by benevolent dictators, some by not-so-benevolent dictators. But these dictators—bosses, managers, whatever you want to call them—have businesses to run, and they can pretty much fire the hired help for almost any reason beyond race, color, and creed type of stuff. They can send employees packing for saying they like sunny days or corn flakes or anything else. CBS News sure could have fired me for accusing the media elites of slanting the news.

But what about what constitutional scholars like Harvard professor Alan Dershowitz have called "the spirit of free speech"?

John Rocker, the Atlanta Braves pitcher, didn't have any free-speech rights to say the subway ride to Shea Stadium in New York was like driving through Beirut ... or to describe the passengers as "some kid with purple hair, next to some queer with AIDS, right next to some dude who just got out of jail for the fourth time, right next to some twenty-year-old mom with four kids."

In terms of keeping his job, he had no free-speech right to say, "The biggest thing I don't like about New York are the foreigners." The government couldn't shut him up—but the Braves sure could. They could have unloaded Rocker in less time than it takes his fastball to reach home plate.

But in a *New York Times* op-ed, Dershowitz pointed out, "The Constitution may impose limits only on the government, but the First Amendment is premised on the idea that there should be a free marketplace of ideas. Private universities, for example, are not constrained by the Constitution, but most choose to follow it anyway, because they recognize that the exchange of ideas—no matter how wrongheaded or obnoxious—is good for education."

You'd think the media would look at it the same way.

In my case, which came a few years before Rocker, wouldn't it have been just a tad hypocritical for CBS News, which is allowed to say unpopular things about any subject under the sun precisely because of the First Amendment, to fire me for expressing my own "unpopular" views? But Klein let me know that if I became a sympathetic character at CBS News's expense, if I encouraged writers to support me, the company would use "all the big guns in its arsenal" against me.

"All the big guns in its arsenal!" What the hell did that mean? That's what Carlo Gambino says to Crazy Joey Gallo. But there was no rancor in Jon's voice. None. It was simply a friendly piece of advice. Klein, of course, was talking about a public relations arsenal. CBS, like all big companies, has people on the payroll who do things like that. They could plant stories with friendly newspaper writers about how I had to go because no one would work with me in the wake of the op-ed column, or, who knows, maybe that I was "a political activist with a political agenda."

"That's how corporations do things," Klein said, nonchalantly. "You know that."

Forget the Gambinos and the Gallos—*forget the Sopranos*—this was the stuff of the Corleones. Mario Puzo was writing the script; Jon Klein was merely delivering it. Jon was Al Pacino playing Michael. The calm one. The smart one. The one who, like Klein, was an Ivy League guy. The one who, when push came to shove, would have his own brother knocked off. Only a fool wouldn't get Klein's message: You hurt us . . . and we hurt you. A hundred times over. We use all the big guns in the arsenal to hurt you.

I understood this was nothing personal. Just business.

Not long after the op-ed was published, Andrew Heyward called me at home in Miami, where I was spending most of my days since I had no job to go to, and summoned me to his office in New York. We met late in the afternoon. Jon Klein was there.

"Will you apologize to the entire staff of CBS News?" Heyward asked.

"No, I will not," I told him. I would be willing to apologize to Engberg "if I hurt his feelings." But that was it. I was sticking by what I wrote.

To his credit, Heyward didn't push the issue; he didn't make a company-wide apology a condition for me to keep my job.

A few weeks later I did apologize to Engberg, in a note, saying my intent was never to hurt him or his family or his friends in the Washington bureau of CBS News. And if I did, I said, I was sorry. But the issue, I made clear, was journalism. "Someday, soon I hope, I will stop being the issue," I wrote Engberg. "I do think it's convenient for some to focus attention on the messenger—why not?—it conveniently deflects attention from the message. Someday I hope serious people will discuss the serious point I made. Some will agree; others won't. That's OK. But the issue should never be that 'Goldberg launched a personal attack on Engberg.' ... My point was about journalism and I stand by it. It was never about personalities or personal shots."

Engberg, whose last words to me had been "You're full of shit," never responded to my apology. Not to me, anyway. But he did contact my boss and his, Andrew Heyward, to say that he would not accept this or any other "self-serving" apology, so long as I continued to stand by what I had written in the *Wall Street Journal*.

The meeting in New York, with Heyward and Klein, didn't last long. They offered no hints as to what they were going to do with me. But it looked like my problems weren't going away anytime soon. Because not only would I continue to stand by what I had written, I was more convinced than ever that I was right.

They were all protesting entirely too much.

A letter to Ann Landers was making its way around CBS News.

"Dear Ann: I have a problem. I have two brothers. One brother is in television, the other was put to death in the electric chair for murder.

My mother died from insanity when I was three years old. My sisters are prostitutes, and my father sells narcotics to high school students. Recently I met a girl who was just released from a reformatory where she served time for smothering her illegitimate child to death, and I want to marry her.

"My problem is—if I marry this girl, should I tell her about my brother who is in television?"

Not a bad question.

The letter to Ann Landers is parody, of course. The interview Dan Rather gave Tom Snyder only sounds like parody.

Rather doesn't believe there is a liberal bias in the news. That's why he went on Tom Snyder's late-night TV show on February 8, 1995, and said, "It's one of the great political myths, about press bias. Most reporters don't know whether they're Republican or Democrat, and vote every which way."

When Dan says something as breathtakingly goofy as that you have to wonder—is the boy just toying with us or does he really believe it? *"Most reporters don't know if they're Republican or Democrat"?* On what planet, Dan, would that be?

"...and vote every which way"? I don't think so. They vote over-whelmingly Democratic. Could Dan Rather really be the only person in the entire United States of America who doesn't know this?

Most reporters, though, aren't as defensive as Dan. They take a more seductive position. Even if we are liberal, they say, so what? As long as we keep our biases out of the stories we cover, what's the difference how we feel about abortion or gun control or anything else?

They're right. Completely and totally 100 percent right. And perhaps on Planet Bizarro in some parallel universe their personal views about life and the world really wouldn't matter. But they do here on Earth, because, even though some would take issue, reporters and editors really are only human, which means they bring all their biases and life experiences to their stories.

And it shows.

Look at it this way: Imagine that almost all of the people who bring you the news on CBS and NBC and ABC voted for Richard Nixon over George McGovern, instead of the other way around. Imagine that they favored Ronald Reagan over Walter Mondale. Now imagine that the media elites are mostly *against* affirmative action and mostly *for* the death penalty. Pretend that most network journalists are *for* prayer in the public schools and *against* a woman's right to have an abortion.

Now make believe that they broadcast the news each night, not from Manhattan, the most liberal enclave in America (except maybe for Hollywood and a few college towns), but from Omaha, Nebraska. Imagine, too, that their neighbors are not highly paid, sophisticated New Yorkers who, like the media elites, send their children to expensive private schools in Manhattan with the overwhelmingly white sons and daughters of other wealthy, sophisticated New Yorkers—even as they bemoan how segregated by race and class America remains.

Imagine instead that they send their kids to the Omaha public schools, where their children sit next to mostly middle-class boys and girls whose parents aren't big shots in the world of high finance and law and journalism, but mostly work in less glamorous jobs at Mutual of Omaha or at the county courthouse or on a farm or maybe even at the hardware store.

Do we really think that if the media elites worked out of Nebraska instead of New York, and if they were overwhelmingly social conservatives instead of liberals, and if they overwhelmingly voted for Nixon and Reagan instead of McGovern and Mondale...do we really think that would make no difference? Does anyone really believe that the evening newscasts would fundamentally be the same?

Sure, they'd still cover tornadoes and plane crashes pretty much the same way, but do we really think they'd cover abortion and affirmative action and gay rights the same way? Or would their conservatism, reinforced by their surroundings, their friends and neighbors, somehow—in some vague, subtle way—influence how they see the world and how they report the news?

Maybe these make-believe conservative journalists would be more open-minded if there were some diversity in their lives. So, just to make sure that we don't become too parochial out there on the plains, we would make sure that we had racial, ethnic, and gender diversity at our new network broadcast centers in Omaha. We would make sure that our news organizations were populated not just with white male conservatives but also with black male conservatives and Hispanic and Asian male conservatives and black and Hispanic and Asian women conservatives, too.

Do we think that because we have this wonderful diversity, this magnificent rainbow coalition, that we would get a less narrow, less biased, and more honest newscast?

Why does it look so patently ridiculous, so obviously silly, when the tables are turned, when conservatives are in the majority? Why don't the people who run the networks in New York think it's just as ridiculous, just as silly, and just as harmful to have such a disproportionate number of liberals, no matter what their color or gender or ethnic background, giving us the news each night?

Does anyone think a "diverse" group of conservative journalists would give us the news straight? I sure as hell don't. They'd be just like the Left. Except, they'd let their *conservative* biases slip into the news, and they'd swear on a stack of Bibles that they were mainstream . . . just as liberals do now.

It's the human condition.

Is it possible that conservative reporters just might have a tendency to go to Phyllis Schlafly and other conservative women to get "mainstream" women's reactions to stories, instead of going to the women from NOW as liberals in the media tend to do?

Could it be that conservative journalists might not see any bias in describing liberal Democrats like Barney Frank or Dick Gephardt as "bombastic and ruthless," the exact words that Eric Engberg used November 2, 1994, to describe Newt Gingrich on Dan Rather's *CBS Evening News*?

Do you think there might be more stories about religion if there were more conservative journalists running America's newsrooms?

No conspiracies. No deliberate attempts to slant the news. It just happens. Because the way reporters and editors see the world, the way their friends and colleagues see the world, matters.

In their book *The Media Elite*, Robert and Susan Lichter along with Stanley Rothman ask the fundamental question: "What do journalists' backgrounds have to do with their work? In general, the way we were brought up and the way we live shape our view of the world."

It sounds fairly obvious. News, after all, isn't just a collection of facts. It's also how reporters and editors see those facts, how they interpret them, and most important, what facts they think are newsworthy to begin with.

So if long ago we came to the conclusion that newsrooms with too many white men were a bad idea because all we got was the white male perspective, then why isn't it just as bad to have so many liberals dominating the culture of the newsroom?

Inevitably, they see the world a certain way, from a liberal perspective— a world where money is often seen as a solution to social problems, where anti-abortionists are seen as kooks and weirdos, where groups, not just individuals, have rights—and because that's how they see things, that's also how they report the news.

None of this would matter, of course, if Dan Rather were right when he told Tom Snyder that "most reporters don't know whether they're Republican or Democrat, and vote every which way [and] . . . would fall in the general category of kind of commonsense moderates." Because if this business that says reporters are a bunch of liberals who almost always vote Democratic is a "myth," as Dan put it, and if this "myth" was concocted by a bunch of right-wingers to make journalists look bad, then this whole issue of liberal bias would just be a "canard," to use another of Dan's words.

"This is basically a canard used by politicians, and I understand why," he told a caller on the Snyder show. "Because they want to blame somebody, anybody but themselves, for people's anger and frustration."

There's some truth there. Some right-wing ideologues do blame "the liberal news media" for everything from crime to cancer. But that doesn't detract from another truth: that, by and large, the media elites really are liberal. And Democrats, too. And both affect their news judgment.

None of this should be seen as an argument against liberal values, or as an endorsement of conservative values. This is a big country with a lot of people, and there's room for all sorts of views. This is nothing more than an argument for fairness and balance, something liberals ought to care about as much as conservatives, because if by some unimaginable series of events, conservatives wind up in control of not just a cable network here or there, but hundreds of America's newsrooms, then, if history is any guide, they will slant the news to *their* liking. And the Left in this country will scream about how unfair things are—and they will be right. But they ought to realize that that's how reasonable, honest conservatives feel today.

On December 6, 1998, on a *Meet the Press* segment about Bill Clinton and his relationship with the Washington news corps, one of the capital's media stars, the *Washington Post*'s Sally Quinn, felt she needed to state what to her was the obvious.

The Washington press corps, she insisted, was not some "monolith." "We all work for different organizations," she said, "we all think differently."

Not really, Sally.

Two years earlier, in 1996, the Freedom Forum and the Roper Center released the results of a now famous survey of 139 Washington bureau chiefs and congressional correspondents. The results make you wonder what in the world Sally Quinn was talking about.

The Freedom Forum is an independent foundation that examines issues that involve the media. The Roper Center is an opinion research firm, also with a solid reputation. "No way that the data are the fruit of right-wing press bashers," as the journalist Ben Wattenberg put it.

What these two groups found was that Washington journalists are far more liberal and far more Democratic than the typical American voter:

- 89 percent of the journalists said they voted for Bill Clinton in 1992, compared with just 43 percent of the nonjournalist voters.
- 7 percent of the journalists voted for George Bush; 37 percent of the voters did.
- 2 percent of the news people voted for Ross Perot while 19 percent of the electorate did.

Eighty-nine percent voted for Bill Clinton. This is incredible when you think about it. There's hardly a candidate in the entire United States of America who carries his or her district with 89 percent of the vote. This is way beyond mere landslide numbers. The only politicians who get numbers like that are called Fidel Castro or Saddam Hussein. The same journalists that Sally Quinn tells us do not constitute a "monolith" certainly vote like one.

Sally says they "all think differently." About what? Picking the best appetizer at the Ethiopian restaurant in Georgetown?

What party do journalists identify with?

- 50 percent said they were Democrats.
- *4 percent* said they were Republicans.

When they were asked, "How do you characterize your political orientation?" 61 percent said "liberal" or "moderate to liberal." Only 9 percent said they were "conservative" or "moderate to conservative."

In the world of media elites, Democrats outnumber Republicans by twelve to one and liberals outnumber conservatives by seven to one. Yet Dan Rather believes that "most reporters don't know whether they're Republican or Democrat, and vote every which way." In your dreams, Dan.

After the survey came out, the *Washington Post* media writer, Howard Kurtz, said on *Fox News Sunday*, "Clearly anybody looking at those numbers, if they're even close to accurate, would conclude that there is a diversity problem in the news business, and it's not just the kind of diversity we usually talk about, which is not getting enough minorities in the news business, but political diversity, as well. Anybody who doesn't see that is just in denial."

James Glassman put it this way in the *Washington Post*: "The people who report the stories are liberal Democrats. This is the shameful open secret of American journalism. That the press itself . . . chooses to gloss over it is conclusive evidence of how pernicious the bias is."

Tom Rosenstiel, the director of the Project for Excellence in Journalism, says, "Bias is the elephant in the living room. We're in denial about it and don't want to admit it's there. We think it's less of a problem than the public does, and we just don't want to get into it."

Even *Newsweek*'s Evan Thomas (the one who thought Ronald Reagan had "a kind of intuitive idiot genius") has said, "There is a liberal bias. It's demonstrable. You look at some statistics. About 85 percent of the reporters who cover the White House vote Democratic; they have for a long time. There is a, particularly at the networks, at the lower levels, among the editors and the so-called infrastructure, there is a liberal bias."

Nonsense!

That's the response from Elaine Povich, who wrote the Freedom Forum report. No way, she said, that the survey confirms any liberal bias in the media.

"One of the things about being a professional," she said, "is that you attempt to leave your personal feelings aside as you do your work," she told the *Washington Times*.

"More people who are of a liberal persuasion go into reporting because they believe in the ethics and the ideals," she continued. "A lot of conservatives go into the private sector, go into Wall Street, go into banking. You find people who are idealistic tending toward the reporting end."

"Right," says Ben Wattenberg in his syndicated column. "These ethical, idealistic journalists left their personal feelings aside to this extent: When queried [in the Freedom Foundation/Roper poll in 1996] whether the 1994 Contract with America was an 'election-year campaign ploy' rather than 'a serious reform proposal,' 59 percent said 'ploy' and only 3 percent said 'serious.'"

It's true that only 139 Washington journalists were polled, but there's no reason to think the results were a fluke. Because this wasn't the first survey that showed how liberal so many journalists are.

A poll back in 1972 showed that of those reporters who voted, 70 percent went for McGovern, the most liberal presidential nominee in recent memory, while 25 percent went for Nixon—the same Richard Nixon who carried every single state in the union except Massachusetts.

In 1985 the *Los Angeles Times* conducted a nationwide survey of about three thousand journalists and the same number of people in the general public to see how each group felt about the major issues of the day:

■ 23 percent of the public said they were liberal; 55 percent of the journalists described themselves as liberal.

■ 56 percent of the public favored Ronald Reagan; 30 percent of the journalists favored Reagan.

■ 49 percent of the public was for a woman's right to have an abortion; 82 percent of the journalists were pro-choice.

■ 74 percent of the public was for prayer in public schools; 25 percent of the journalists surveyed were for prayer in the public schools.

■ 56 percent of the nonjournalists were for affirmative action; 81 percent of the journalists were for affirmative action.

■ 75 percent of the public was for the death penalty in murder cases; 47 percent of the journalists were for the death penalty.

■ Half the public was for stricter handgun controls; 78 percent of the journalists were for tougher gun controls.

A more recent study, released in March 2000, also came to the conclusion that journalists are different from most of the people they cover. Peter Brown, an editor at the *Orlando Sentinel* in Florida, did a mini-census of 3,400 journalists and found that they are less likely to get married and have children, less likely to do volunteer community service, less likely to own homes, and less likely to go to church than others who live in the communities where they work.

"How many members of the *Los Angeles Times* and the *St. Louis Post-Dispatch*," he asks, "belong to the American Legion or the Kiwanis or go to prayer breakfasts?"

But it's not just that so many journalists are so different from mainstream America. It's that some are downright hostile to what many Americans hold sacred.

On April 14, 1999, I sat in on a *CBS Weekend News* conference call from a speakerphone in the Miami bureau. It's usually a routine call with CBS News producers all over the country taking part, telling the show producers in New York about the stories coming up in their territories that weekend. Roxanne Russell, a longtime producer out of the Washington bureau, was telling about an event that Gary Bauer would be attending. Bauer was the conservative, family-values activist who seven days later would announce his candidacy for the Republican nomination for president.

Bauer was no favorite of the cultural Left, who saw him as an annoying right-wing moralist. Anna Quindlen, the annoying left-wing moralist and columnist who writes for *Newsweek*, once called him "a man best known for trying to build a bridge to the 19th century."

So maybe I shouldn't have been surprised by what I heard next, but I was. Without a trace of timidity, without any apparent concern for potential consequences, Roxanne Russell, sitting at a desk inside the CBS News Washington bureau, nonchalantly referred to this conservative activist as "Gary Bauer, the little nut from the Christian group."

The little nut from the Christian group!

Those were her exact words, uttered at exactly 12:36 P.M. If any of the CBS News producers on the conference call were shocked, not one of them gave a clue. Roxanne Russell had just called Gary Bauer, the head of a major group of American Christians, "the little nut from the Christian group" and merrily went on with the rest of her list of events CBS News in Washington would be covering.

What struck me was not the obvious disrespect for Bauer. Journalists, being as terribly witty and sophisticated as we are, are always putting someone down. Religious people are especially juicy targets. In a lot of newsrooms, they're seen as odd and viewed with suspicion because their lives are shaped by faith and devotion to God and an adherence to rigid principles—opposition to abortion, for one—that seem archaic and closed-minded to a lot of journalists who, survey after survey suggests, are not especially religious themselves.

So it wasn't the hostility to Bauer in and of itself that threw me. It was the lack of concern of any kind in showing that disrespect *so openly*. Producers from CBS News bureaus all over the country were on the phone. And who knows who else was listening, just as I was.

So I wondered: would a network news producer ever make such a disparaging remark, so openly, about the head of a Jewish group? Or a gay group? Or a black group?

"Tomorrow we'll be covering that pro-Israel lobby and Sam Schwartz, the little nut from the Jewish group, will be there."

Or how about this: *"We'll be covering that gay parade on Saturday and Billy Smith, the little fag from the gay group, will be leading it."*

Or try this one: *"There's a rally at the Washington Monument this weekend and Jesse Jackson, the big nut from that black group, will be there."*

Anything even resembling that kind of talk would be grounds for instant dismissal. But calling a prominent Christian "the little nut" is no big deal!

Nor was it any big deal, to Ted Turner anyway, when he once said that Christianity was a religion "for losers," a remark he later apologized for. But that didn't stop him on Ash Wednesday 2001 from sharing more of his wit and wisdom about Christians. Turner was at the CNN bureau in Washington when he noticed that several of his news people had ashes on their foreheads, and it apparently left him befuddled.

"I was looking at this woman and I was trying to figure out what was on her forehead," Turner was quoted as saying. "At first I thought you were in the [Seattle] earthquake, but I realized you're just Jesus freaks."

Coming from someone else, who knows, it might have been taken as nothing more than—to use the catch phrase of the day—an "inappropriate" attempt to be funny. But given the religion "for losers" comment a decade earlier, some Catholic groups understandably were not laughing. When the news got out, Turner again apologized, calling his remark "thoughtless."

But if anyone on the CBS News conference call that day thought the shot at Gary Bauer was thoughtless, you wouldn't know it by the silence. Despite its thirst for diversity, despite years of hiring people to reflect the diversity of America, there apparently wasn't a single producer at CBS News who heard Roxanne's shot at "the little nut from the Christian group" who would stand up and say "this is wrong." I sure as hell couldn't complain. I had made waves three long years earlier, and I was still in the doghouse for it.

So what's a news organization to do? CBS can't have producers running around taking nasty little shots at conservatives who head up Christian organizations, can it? And what about that other disturbing little problem, the one about reporters who seem blissfully detached from the very people watching and reading their news reports?

What to do?

How about some good old-fashioned affirmative action?

Since the *Los Angeles Times* survey shows that more than eight out of ten journalists favor affirmative action for women and minorities, maybe they could get behind an affirmative action program for another underrepresented minority: conservatives in the world of journalism.

Too crazy? Newsroom liberals would never accept it? How do we know?

The polls say they love affirmative action. They think people who are against it are Neanderthals at best and downright bigots at worst. Besides, we're not calling for quotas. That would be wrong. Just some goals and timetables to bring more conservatives into America's newsrooms.

An affirmative action plan for conservative journalists might bring some real diversity to the newsroom, not the make-believe kind we have now. And while we would tell these conservatives to leave their political and ideological baggage at the door (*just as I'm sure liberal journalists have been told for years—ya think?*), we should welcome the different perspective they would bring to the job of reporting the news.

Of course, in an ideal world, we wouldn't need conservatives to balance liberals. In an ideal world, we wouldn't ask, no matter how subtly, if a prospective hire was conservative or liberal. In an ideal world, none of this would matter. But obviously we don't live in an ideal world. That's why we have affirmative action. Right?

News executives are always saying we need our staffs to look more like the real America. How about if those reporters and editors and executives also *thought* just a little more like the real America? And shared just a little more of their values? And brought just a little more of *their* perspective to the job?

Nahhhh! It's definitely too crazy! The journalists who love affirmative action would hate it.

Targeting Men 9

P *utz.*

It's one of those funny-sounding, completely inelegant Yiddish words that is totally without charm but manages to make its point.

Like *schmuck.*

For the uninitiated, *putz,* loosely translated, means jerk—as in "I went to this fabulously trendy East Side restaurant and ordered the pesto pasta with sun-dried tomatoes and the waiter brought me spaghetti and meatballs. What a *putz!*"

For some reason this word is used a lot in Manhattan but almost never in Jackson Hole, Wyoming. As for the literal translation of *putz*—don't ask. (Hint: rhymes with Venus.)

Putz probably had its heyday during the 1998 New York Senate race, when Republican Al D'Amato called his Democratic opponent, Charles Schumer, a *"putz*head," a witty variation on the original *"putz"*—perhaps not in the Oscar Wilde or George Bernard Shaw class of sophisticated observations, but no one ever confused Al D'Amato with Oscar Wilde or George Bernard Shaw.

Such uncivil behavior caught the ever watchful eye of the *New York Times* editorial page, which said such language epitomized D'Amato's nastiness and vitriol. The *Times* also noted that New Yorkers who in the past might have voted for D'Amato rejected him in 1998, at least in part because of the "wounding power of slurs."

The "wounding power of slurs" is something the *New York Times* and sensitive network news types are always on the lookout for. Except when the slur is aimed at the one group they consider fair game.

Men.

This brings us to Harry Smith, the former coanchor of *CBS This Morning*, as affable a feminist as you'll ever meet—and even in a business populated by so many liberals, Harry is out there, way off in left field. It was the summer of 1995, August 14, to be exact. I had just come back from a vacation in Alaska with my wife, Nancy, and our daughter, Catherine. We were at a hotel in Seattle, and I turned on *CBS This Morning* to see what was going on.

There was Harry interviewing the actor Dennis Quaid about a movie he had just done, *Something to Talk About*. In the movie Quaid plays a sleazeball, a married man who can't keep his hands off half the women in town.

To Harry this is how men act in real life too. Which prompted him to say to Quaid, "I'm under the assumption that most men are *putzes*."

In Harry's mind this was a perfectly reasonable observation. Because to Harry Smith, most men *are* putzes. I know this because I called him a few days later and asked just what he had in mind.

"Men are the cheaters," Harry told me. "Men are the philanderers. We're the ones who don't take care of our families."

The word *putz* was creeping into my mind . . . but it wasn't "*most men*" I was thinking about.

"And white guys are running around the country complaining that *they're* victims," he added, just to make sure I was getting his point.

I understand all that but what I can't figure out is how you can spell "Harry Smith" without using the letters pc.

But what if affable Harry Smith (who in 1999 left CBS News to host A&E's *Biography*) in some other context had said, "I'm under the assumption that most black people are *putzes*"? Or "most Irish are *putzes*"? Or "most Jews are *putzes*"?

Let's put it this way: if he had said any of those things, good ol' Harry would have been out on his affable liberal ass in about the time it would have taken his bosses to say, "Pack your stuff and get out, you *putz!*" Even then, Harry would have been lucky to get a job doing the overnight news at a radio station in Kodiak, Alaska, which is one of those places where they don't use the word *putz* all that much.

"What if you said on the air," I asked Harry, "you know, I think most *women* are *putzes*. Do you think management would have tolerated that?"

He couldn't stop laughing. What Harry meant is, *"You've got to be kidding, putzhead—they would have tossed me out the freakin' window."*

Nobody at CBS News thought this *putz* episode was any big deal. Eric Ober, the president of the news division, said it was a joke. No harm, no foul.

I'm sure he was right. And I'm sure he would have felt the same way if I had gone on television and said, "You know, Ms. Steinem, I don't understand what you and all your feminist friends are always complaining about. You women are such *putzes*."

And it was a joke, too, when Katie Couric, on NBC, asked a bride who had been jilted at the altar about a proper remedy: "Have you considered castration as an option?"

Warren Farrell, a California psychologist and former board member of the New York chapter of NOW, was exercising at his home near San Diego, watching the *Today* show, the morning Katie made her castration joke. In his book, *Women Can't Hear What Men Don't Say*, he wondered what would happen if Katie's cohost, Matt Lauer, asked a jilted groom, "Have you considered the option of cutting off her breasts?"

Well, Farrell didn't really wonder what would happen. Like everybody else, he knew. "NBC would be considering the option of cutting off his contract."

The difference between the two is obvious, isn't it? Castration is funny. Cutting off breasts is not funny.

But Warren Farrell was on to something. An executive at CBS News—who doesn't want his name attached to such an un-PC idea—calls it the "License to Overkill."

"Any group that feels, rightly or wrongly, that it has been oppressed, no matter how much or how little, has the license to overkill," he told me. "It's sort of like James Bond's 007 license. But that's just a license to kill.

"Once you have the license to overkill you can say just about anything you want about the oppressors. And get away with it."

The *New York Times*—the paper that worries about the "wounding power of slurs"—apparently possesses this 007-plus license.

Take a story by *Times* reporter Natalie Angier that begins this way: "Women may not find this surprising, but one of the most persistent and frustrating problems in evolutionary biology is the male. Specifically... why doesn't he just go away?"

Or how about this story by the same Ms. Angier: "Today is Father's Day.... We women are supposed to... make them feel like princes while letting them act like turnips.

"The section you are reading is about women's health. And so what better place to address the question: Are they worth it?... Do we live better with men or without them?"

Men should not lose their sense of humor as some feminists have. This is what passes for clever at the *Times*. But what if she had written that blacks commit a disproportionate amount of violent street crime, make up a disproportionate number of inmates in our prisons, and because of that, drain tax dollars that might otherwise go to libraries and museums and homeless shelters?

"Are they worth it? Do we live better with blacks or without them?"

The reason one question is supposed to be legitimate and the other isn't is that blacks (or gays or women) haven't lived the life of privilege and power that (white) men supposedly have. The License to Overkill lets Ms. Angier and the *Times* ask dopey questions about whether men "are worth it" but would never allow someone to ask another bigoted question about whether blacks are worth it.

Sometimes it's important to state the obvious: Not all men—not even all white men—have power and privilege. Some work in corner offices on the fiftieth floor, and some work in coal mines and fast food restaurants. But it's that kind of shallow, stereotypical thinking that leads to shoddy journalism when it comes to serious gender issues that affect men.

Even Sam Donaldson, one of the toughest reporters in all of television journalism, turns into a sniveling wimp when it comes to challenging feminists.

A while back, Donaldson wrote in his autobiography, *Hold On, Mr. President!*, "because of me no one gets a free ride." Well, almost no one. Once Sam called a female park ranger a "rangerette" and got so many complaints from angry feminists that years later, he tells us, he "failed to ask a single challenging, provocative question of leaders of feminist organizations" regarding a controversial rape story. "I've been very careful about offending women," he writes. "I'll challenge presidents any day, but taking on half the world is asking too much."

Nice going, *putz*!

Asa Baber, who writes the "Men" column for *Playboy* picked up on Sam's wimpiness.

"I am here to invite you, whenever you get the balls, to join me in challenging the excesses of feminism, Sam." The problem, Baber pointed out, is that if you feel intimidated by feminists, if you really believe they in fact have a license to overkill, then you're going to take a dive on a whole range of serious issues that affect men—and their wives and children.

"Who among the...presidential candidates of the past two decades," Baber asks, "has spoken boldly about men's rights? Who has even used the phrase? Who has represented us on the presidential stump in the areas of divorce, child custody, abortion, military-draft registration, false accusations of rape, high unemployment for both young and old men, male longevity and health, discrimination against men in the workplace and in the culture?"

If the big-time media elites weren't such feminists themselves, or afraid of offending them, they might have done some fresh, interesting stories on a whole range of gender issues instead of the old "safe" clichés.

We've done a million stories at the networks on deadbeat dads—fair enough—but almost none on how too many divorced women use custody and visitation as weapons to punish their ex-husbands for what went wrong during the marriage.

It's true enough that some men really are deadbeats. But the deadbeat dad stories we often do are about those rich doctors and businessmen who would rather spend their money on convertibles and speedboats and young blondes than on their own children. That happens, but it's not typical. The real story is that a lot of men who don't pay support are poor; they hold menial jobs; they're undereducated. Many of them pay when they can.

Journalists, and liberals in general, should care about poor men like that. But to the media elites—being as reliably feminist as they are—the very idea that men in divorce and custody cases might be part of an oppressed class is an alien concept. So only occasionally do we tiptoe near a story about the millions of divorced dads who want to maintain a strong relationship with their kids but are kept away by angry moms.

As long as the media elites let feminists from the Left define the issue, they will always see men as the bad guys, as the *putzes* of America.

And that's why we won't see stories that ask why, after more than thirty years of modern feminism, we still have laws saying that only eighteen-year-old *men* have to sign up with Selective Service, in case the government reinstates the military draft. Young women do not.

We get entire segments on the news about breast cancer—but hardly a word about prostate cancer.

We see tons of stories about how women don't earn as much as men in the workplace—but we see virtually nothing on the evening news about *why* there's a difference. In *Women Can't Hear What Men Don't Say,* Warren Farrell tells us.

Men do indeed earn more, he says, "but for *very different work* (more hazardous jobs, more technical professions like engineering or brain surgeon, etc.), *very different behavior at work* (longer hours, working night shifts, etc.), and *very different efforts to obtain the work* (working in much less enticing locations [Alaskan oil rigs, coal mines], commuting further, relocating more, working overseas), and so on."

And why haven't reporters asked the commonsense question that Farrell asked me when we spoke: "If women really earned 59 cents [or whatever it supposedly is up to now] to the dollar for the same work as men, how could a business compete with its competition by hiring men *at any level*?" In other words, wouldn't all businesses hire *only* women if everything else was the same, and they really did work for less money?

By constantly portraying women as second-class citizens, as helpless victims of the all-powerful, oppressive, white-male power structure, a certain image of men is created. And it's not particularly sympathetic.

But if all this had no effect in the real world, if it simply were a matter of CBS News being tone deaf when Harry Smith says most men are *putzes* and NBC not caring when Katie Couric jokes about castration, it would only be annoying.

But images really do count, even in such seemingly small, unimportant matters. The way we portrayed women in the media—cleaning toilet bowls in those old black-and-white TV commercials, grinning like children when their much smarter husbands let them drive the new '55 Olds—shaped not only the way we saw women, but the way we treated them, even if way back then almost no one found anything particularly offensive about the images.

It's the same with men today.

In 1998 I covered a story that would have sent shivers down Kafka's spine, a story about a feminist politician, whose bureaucracy was running amok and ruining innocent lives.

It was happening in Los Angeles, where men—no one knew for sure how many—were being forced to pay child support, for up to eighteen years, *for children that everyone agreed were not theirs!*

Gil Garcetti, then the district attorney of Los Angeles County, a politician with strong ties to southern California feminists, was on a very public crusade to make deadbeat dads pay up. Except that the bureaucracy went haywire and completely innocent men were caught in Gil Garcetti's dragnet.

One of them was a young man named John Johnson, who received in the mail a court order to pay $7,000 in delinquent support for a child he had no relationship to whatsoever. The official papers had Johnson's name and address right, but everything else on the paper was wrong. The John Johnson that Garcetti was looking for had a different social security number and a different driver's license number. This man I was talking to clearly was not a deadbeat dad. The bureaucrats had the wrong John Johnson.

The bureaucrats' reaction: tough luck.

"I've been making phone calls," John Johnson told me, "I've been complaining. I've been sending letters. They don't respond. My question is: What do they do to protect against picking the wrong people with common names like mine? What do they do? Can they just go after anybody and nobody's accountable? There's something wrong. There's something wrong with that department."

Then there was Walter Vollmer, a German immigrant who settled in southern California with his wife Christina thirty years ago. One day, Vollmer went to his mailbox and found a bill for back child support... *$206,000 of back child support!*

"Apparently there is some other Walter Vollmer around," his lawyer, Craig Elkin, told me. "And my only guess at this point is that they found a Walter Vollmer in Los Angeles County, and they figured, 'How many can there be? Let's send the bill to him.'"

For months Vollmer couldn't fix the problem. He couldn't convince any of the bureaucrats they had the wrong man. His wife, a proper woman with old-world sensibilities, was starting to wonder if he had been leading a secret life.

"I was frightened," she told me. Could the government really be so wrong? she kept wondering. How could it continue to send her husband bills month after month unless he really did have a mysterious child somewhere? Maybe, she admits thinking, he had a second wife hidden away someplace. The pressure was so great they almost divorced after thirty-one years of marriage.

Finally, his lawyer convinced Gil Garcetti that he had made a mistake. But other men weren't nearly so lucky.

Tony Jackson, a working-class black man with a wife and two kids, got a bill from Gil Garcetti's deadbeat dad squad saying he owed $13,000 in back child support for a child that, he would soon prove, was not his.

Jackson took a DNA test at a lab the court picked. It showed he was definitely not the father.

Tough luck.

The law says anyone who receives an official court notice saying he owes child support has thirty days to respond—thirty days!—and if you don't respond in thirty days, you're considered "in default" and must pay support—*until the child is eighteen.*

Jackson was named by a woman he used to date, who, in order to qualify for welfare, had to name *somebody* as the father of her child. So she picked Tony Jackson, even though he wasn't the father. Jackson didn't respond to the court order within thirty days, because he swears he never got the notice. He says he learned about it after it was sent to a former employer who never forwarded it to him. Still, he was ordered to pay child support for a child everyone, even Gil Garcettti, agreed was not his.

When I met Tony Jackson, he was a wreck. On the verge of suicide, I feared. He cried during our conversation. He said he couldn't take his own two kids out to a restaurant for a meal. He couldn't afford it, because the court was taking the child support out of his paycheck before he ever got it.

Jackson finally got a lawyer, Louis Dell, who told me, "The district attorney has a win-at-all-costs attitude. It's unconscionable. We have the benefit of very accurate genetic blood testing. It tells us what the truth is. It tells us that Mr. Jackson is not the father."

It didn't matter.

Jackson didn't respond in time, which put him "in default." So he had to pay child support for someone else's child. He took a second job as a night security guard to make ends meet. This left him less time to spend with his own children.

"It's a dark alley," Tony Jackson told me while trying, without much success, to hold back his tears. "There's no light at the end of the tunnel."

When I told Gil Garcetti about this, at his offices in downtown Los Angeles, he was straightforward and unsympathetic.

"It's very simple. If you don't respond to the court's summons and no one ever shows up in court for you, we will get a default judgment against you. It's that simple. I am out there to try and collect as much money as

I can for the children, for the custodial mother who is on welfare or who barely has enough money to stay off welfare. I'm going to do that."

But why not just say, "Look, you're clearly not the father, the paternity test has proved it. All right, you don't have to pay"? I asked him.

"That violates the law," was his cold-blooded answer.

Had he ever gone after a mother who falsely named an old boyfriend just to qualify for welfare? Had he ever filed charges against *even one*? No, he said. Not even one. It would be too difficult to prove she was lying, he said. Maybe she had just made an honest mistake.

I also met an undercover Los Angeles police detective who was named the father of an ex-girlfriend's baby and was ordered to pay $14,000 in back support, which the bureaucrats were garnisheeing from his wages, a chunk each week.

"They claim that they served me with a subpoena that I didn't respond to in court," he told me. "And they entered a judgment in default. They said that I was legally the father."

But he also took a DNA test that proved without any doubt he was not the father.

His lawyer, a young woman named Fatima Araiza, was fuming when I spoke to her.

"They've got that judgment against you and it's going to be enforced regardless of all the screaming, the jumping up and down that you do saying, 'Look, I'm not the dad, I'm not the dad, everybody knows I'm not the dad. It's been acknowledged. It's been proven.' And what they're saying is, 'So what?'"

"This is no longer the oppression of women," she said, "this is now the oppression of men. The oppression of responsible men."

What did Garcetti have to say?

"The law is the law."

This was an injustice that could only happen in a culture where men are seen as *putzes* with too much power, especially over women.

But as troubling as the story was, what I found even more disturbing was that even though about ten million Americans watched it on the now defunct CBS News program *Public Eye*, only two called—two men who thought what they had seen was insane.

Had I done a story about a dog that was mistreated, it would have evoked more sympathy—a lot more!—than these men were receiving.

There were no calls from the civil rights establishment, even though many of the victims were poor black and Hispanic men. No calls from the ACLU. No calls from feminists, either, who would rightly have marched on City Hall if the tables had been turned.

Just imagine: a network news story saying there are hundreds of women in Los Angeles County being forced to pay child support for children that are not theirs. Some women were just unlucky enough to have common names like Mary Jones. But others were picked by old boyfriends who had to name someone in order to qualify for welfare. The women took DNA tests ordered by the courts. They proved conclusively they were not the mothers. The district attorney, a man known to embrace men's causes, said, too bad. "The law's the law; they didn't respond to the court order within thirty days."

Can you imagine that? Neither can I.

But this is what happens when simplistic deadbeat dad stories become a staple of American journalism. It creates an atmosphere in which it's easier to accept the notion that once a man has been called a deadbeat, he must be. No matter what the DNA says.

Call men *putzes* on a network news program, and you start to think it's okay to bash them, either with words or with Garcetti-type actions.

Let cute, perky Katie ask a jilted bride if she considered castrating the bum, and the images start to do their work. The message becomes clear: Men are the problem. Isn't that what Natalie Angier of the *New York Times* was writing about when she asked, "Are they worth it? Do we live better with men or without them?"

Add to that odds and ends like a piece from Anna Quindlen who wrote in her old *New York Times* column, "Some of my best friends are men. It is simply that I think women are superior to men." Or a *Times* headline in the book review section that simply states, "Don't Expect Too Much of Men." Or an uncritical CNN story about a book called *How to Make Your Man Behave in 21 Days or Less Using the Secrets of Professional Dog Trainers*.

I know it might seem trivial. I understand the License to Overkill. How it's okay to say anything about the rich and powerful. Except that most men are not rich and powerful. Most men are not CEOs. Certainly not those men in Los Angeles—Tony Jackson, John Johnson, Walter Vollmer, and the undercover LAPD detective.

They know, just as the early feminists knew, that the way journalists portray *any group of people* matters. But if it were just happening in the often silly, superficial world of the media, especially television news, it wouldn't mean all that much. What makes it matter is that male bashing on TV takes a hard toll in the real world.

Any *putz* ought to understand that.

During the Yankees-Mets World Series in 2000, Meredith Vieira of *The View*, the ABC gabfest for women, went to Shea Stadium to make a jackass out of herself.

She went up to Mets slugger Mike Piazza and said, "Let's talk about bats. Who has the biggest wood on the team?" According to Sally Jenkins of the *Washington Post*, who was there, Piazza rolled his eyes.

Vieira also asked one of the other players, "Who's your favorite player to pat on the behind?"

When confronted, Vieira reportedly said, "I'm just having fun," and to Jenkins she claimed, "It was shtick."

"Okay then," Jenkins writes, "for the sake of comedy, for shtick, imagine that Piazza asked Vieira such a question. 'Hey Meredith, who's got the biggest ta-tas?' We would label him a leering pre-Cambrian swine, and throw him to a snarling pack of post-feminists, who would rip his mustache off by the bristles, right? So what do we do with Vieira?"

Good question, Sally. Unfortunately, the answer is nothing. *Absolutely nothing.* Because, except for you, and maybe one or two others, nobody in the mainstream media is going to criticize a feminist. It's against the rules. It's bad form. No one said a word to Harry Smith when he called most men *putzes*, right?

But don't jump to any conclusions about how this proves some kind of hypocritical left-wing media bias. It only looks that way, *putz.*

"Where Thieves and Pimps Run Free" 10

Hunter Thompson, the journalist and author who once ran for sheriff of Aspen on the Freak Power ticket, who only did drugs if they began with a letter of the alphabet, and who consequently was thought (mistakenly) to be a few fries short of a Happy Meal, was never more scathingly perceptive than when he put TV in his crosshairs.

"The TV business is a cruel and shallow money trench, a long plastic hallway where thieves and pimps run free and good men die like dogs."

Whatever we may think of television in America, this much is certain: it's not good when someone who has abused his mind and body as much as Hunter Thompson has comes up with something this honest and brilliant about the medium. It sets a bad example for the kids of America. How can grownups tell them drugs are bad when they see what they've done for Thompson, a man who glided through the 1960s thinking acid was a health food?

However many brain cells Thompson might have lost over the years, in the summer of 1999 his classic description of the TV business was proven true—again. That's when America's oldest and most respected civil rights organization, the NAACP, took a long, hard look down that plastic hallway and didn't like what it saw.

All it could see at CBS, NBC, ABC, and Fox was a cadre of like-minded Moguls—the Titans of Television—the people who shape our pop culture by deciding what gets on the prime-time TV schedule and what doesn't. As far as the NAACP was concerned, these white liberals were behaving like a gang of rednecks decked out in Armanis who might as well have been fronting for David Duke.

NAACP president Kweisi Mfume said the TV business was "the most segregated industry in the United States." Other civil rights leaders accused the Moguls of whitewashing, even ethnic purification. This is the kind of language usually reserved for the Klan and leaders of the Third Reich. Not the Beverly Hills crowd.

What set off the NAACP was the networks' new fall schedules, of all things, which in the view of Kweisi Mfume didn't feature enough black characters (or Hispanic or Asian or other minority characters) in big roles on the networks' sitcoms and dramas.

You can make a case, of course, that instead of complaining the NAACP should have been celebrating. This is how Michael Medved, the mildly conservative social critic with uncommon sense, put it in *USA Today*:

> Imagine for a moment that all of the nation's broadcast executives took boycott and legal threats of NAACP president Kweisi Mfume instantly to heart. They immediately agree to multiply many times over the number of people of color depicted on prime-time TV series. Suddenly, the percentage of black protagonists soars to more than 20 percent—well beyond the 13 percent of the population identified as African-American.

But as part of this happy fantasy, also assume that everything else about network television's offerings remains exactly the same—the same crudeness, rudeness, mindlessness, sniggering sex references, immaturity, exploitation and emphasis on instant gratification. Would merely adjusting the skin color of some prominent characters significantly alter the nature of television itself—and automatically improve its impact on black people?

The Moguls weren't interested in questions like that. What they were interested in was heading off trouble. Boycotts and pickets are bad for business. So even though they tend to dismiss criticism from the Right about how television's "crudeness, rudeness, mindlessness, [and] sniggering sex references" affect the culture, that summer they were far more sympathetic—*and far more fearful!*—of their friends on the Left. So they gave their solemn word as television Moguls to do better.

"This is something we're paying attention to," Fox Entertainment president Doug Herzog somberly announced.

"We realize there's still work to be done," was NBC's earnest reply.

"In May we acknowledged that our new fall programming wasn't as ethnically diverse as we would have liked," was ABC's apologia.

CBS, along with all the other major networks, understandably concerned that their TV studios would be surrounded by pickets chanting, "No Justice, No Peace," promised to add more minority characters to its programs as soon as possible.

What the Moguls did not say, amidst all the promises to do better, was that they're in business to make money, that everything they do in their plastic hallways is about making money, that Hunter Thompson, that troublemaking, acid-popping weirdo had picked just the right words to describe what they already knew: that the TV business really is "a cruel and shallow money trench."

Didn't those NAACP-types understand—the Moguls don't keep blacks off of their sitcoms because they don't like black people? They keep them off the air because they make more money with white people.

In the immortal words of James "Cueball" Carville: "It's the economy, stupid!"

Advertisers like white audiences. They have more money to spend. Robert Johnson, a black Mogul who heads the Black Entertainment Network, said what the white Moguls wouldn't.

"If I'm a network executive, who's probably white . . . and I'm going to launch a show that I think advertisers will like because it will deliver a white audience that the advertisers value more, I'm not going to go and try to do something risky and creative with black people and white people," he said. "I'm certainly going to stay away from black-and-white sex, so that takes out any romance stories involved with black men and white women. I'll probably take out any show that shows a black man as a dynamic businessman, sort of lording over white people, because that's going to offend the angry white male."

TV executives populate their little make-believe world with white stars because they believe that white adults, by and large, would rather watch white stars, by and large—Cosby and Winfrey being more the exceptions that prove the rule.

And there's plenty of evidence to support that belief. I looked at the ratings from Nielsen Media Research for the second quarter of 1999 (March 29–June 27)—just before the NAACP leveled its charges against the networks—and found that almost none of the top shows among black viewers were watched by white viewers—and vice versa:

■ The top program that black viewers watched was *The Steve Harvey Show* on WB. Among whites, it ranked 150th.
■ The number two show among blacks was *For Your Love*, also on WB. It ranked 145th among whites.

■ *The Jamie Foxx Show* (WB) finished third among blacks; it also ranked 145th among whites.

■ *The Wayans Brothers* (WB) was number six with black viewers; 142nd with whites.

And while blacks were watching shows starring black people, whites were watching shows starring white people:

■ The number one show in America among white viewers during the second quarter of 1999 was *Frasier*, the NBC show about two annoyingly effete brothers, both psychiatrists, who know more about Italian art of the Renaissance than they do about the World Series. Among blacks, *Frasier* finished 105th. What a surprise!

■ *ER* was the second biggest show with white viewers. It finished 22nd among blacks.

■ *Friends*, the show about four beautiful white yuppies, finished 3rd with whites, 102nd with blacks.

■ *Veronica's Closet* came in 4th among white viewers, 92nd with blacks.

■ *Will & Grace* was 5th with whites, 112th with blacks.

When it comes to the world of television, especially sitcom television, there really are two Americas—one white, the other black. Except on Monday nights in the fall. *Monday Night Football*, unlike almost every other show on TV, does well with both blacks and whites.

So does *Touched by an Angel*, a show on CBS that seems to touch audiences regardless of race. *Touched by an Angel* features Della Reese, the black singer and actress, as one of several angels who visit people in their daily lives and provide them with spiritual guidance. The show finished seventh in the Nielsens with white viewers, twelfth with blacks.

Program Name	Network	White Rank	Black Rank
Frasier	NBC	1	105
ER	NBC	2	22
Friends	NBC	3	102
Veronica's Closet	NBC	4	92
Will & Grace	NBC	5	112
Home Improvement	ABC	6	64
60 Minutes	CBS	7	26
Touched by an Angel	CBS	7 (tie)	12
Law & Order	NBC	9	17
CBS Sunday Movie	CBS	10	11

Program Name	Network	Black Rank	White Rank
Harvey Show	WB	1	150
For Your Love	WB	2	145
Jamie Foxx	WB	3	145 (tie)
PJ's	FOX	4	108
Walker, Texas Ranger	CBS	5	50
Wayans Brothers	WB	6	143
PJ's (Special)	FOX	7	109
Moesha	UPN	8	105
Smart Guy	WB	9	139
Sons of Thunder	CBS	10	56

Source: Nielsen Media Research/March 29–June 27, 1999

And by early 2001, two new shows crossed the racial divide: *Survivor* and *Who Wants to Be a Millionaire*. *Survivor* finished first among white viewers and seventeenth among blacks. *Millionaire* was third with whites, fourteenth with blacks.

So, is there a lesson here that goes beyond a color-blind fascination with athletes and angels and so-called "reality" and million-dollar game shows? Will blacks and whites—in large numbers—watch a show that features *both* blacks *and* whites? If TV shows were less segregated, would more people watch?

Maybe. In 2001, *Law & Order*, *The Practice*, and *ER*—all smart, well-written dramas with racially mixed casts—finished in the top twenty *with both black and white audiences.*

But what if *Frasier* and Steve Harvey did a show together? What if half the friends on *Friends* were black? Would the audience be much bigger or much smaller? In other words, would more blacks watch *Frasier* and *Friends*—or would fewer whites watch? Or, to put it another way, how much integration is too much integration in the make-believe world of television?

I don't know. But I'm pretty sure about this: We're not about to find out anytime soon. The Moguls won't tamper with success. *Friends* and *Frasier* are gold mines. Bring a few blacks into those neighborhoods, and you run the risk of massive white flight. And that would mean lower ratings, which would mean less ad revenue, which would mean—and this is the really important part—the Moguls could become ex-Moguls overnight. And that—not looking out for Number One—is the only real sin in the plastic hallways where the Moguls conduct the business of television.

So, while the Moguls on the Left Coast support virtually every item on the liberal agenda, while they embrace diversity and affirmative action and deplore segregation in the real world, in the summer of 1999 they stood accused of practicing racial separation in the TV world they controlled. That may make them hypocrites, but does it really make them racists and ethnic purifiers, the way the NAACP meant it?

I don't think so.

If the networks' research departments did studies discovering that ABC, CBS, NBC, and Fox could make more money with black shows than with white shows, the whole fall lineup would look like Harlem. *All* the friends on *Friends* would be black. *Everyone* on *Cheers* would have been black.

If someone discovered that Eskimo shows got bigger ratings and more advertising revenue, the geniuses at the networks would change Frasier's name to Nanook.

ER would be set in Alaska.

They're not bigots, these Titans who control so much of our pop culture. They give money to charity and they love their families. They're just businessmen doing what businessmen do. It's in their nature to make the bottom line the top priority. The color they care most about is green. What could be more American than that?

Unfair?

How else should we explain CBS's shameless decision to put Howard Stern on its owned and operated TV stations on Saturday night? CBS airs Howard Stern because the TV show costs next to nothing to produce and brings in lots of money. So what if the show is filled with farting contests and women shaving their pubic hair? If the Tiffany Network would sink that low for money, it shouldn't surprise anyone that it would toss a few black folks over the side for a single rating point.

This is no bulletin, of course, to anybody who knows how the TV business works. The cultural liberals believe in civil rights as all decent Americans do. They just believe in their own success more. They like living in Beverly Hills and driving new Jaguars and Mercedes. Who wouldn't? And they're not going to give it all up by putting any more blacks (or other minorities) on TV than they absolutely have to.

For what it's worth, a black actor in Los Angeles, Damon Standifer, had a completely different theory on why there are so few blacks on TV. In the *Los Angeles Times* on June 28, 1999, he wrote: "Every type of 'black' show has been protested [by black activists]: If a show portrays wealthy black people, it's criticized for ignoring the plight of poor ones. If a show features poor black people . . . it's criticized for stereotyping black people as poor. . . . In past years there were complaints that the TV show *Seinfeld* never featured a black lead. But honestly, which *Seinfeld* lead could have been cast as an African-American without drawing protests from [black critics]: The spastic, bug-eyed Kramer? The chronically unemployed, lazy George? The sexually promiscuous, self-centered Elaine? Had these characters been black, *Seinfeld* wouldn't have lasted one season."

The Moguls didn't have anything to say about that. But within months, network executives were falling all over themselves adding minority characters to their prime-time lineups. And NBC even promised to add at least one minority writer to any show that survived its first season.

You've got to hand it to the NAACP. It had actually portrayed Hollywood, one of the most liberal communities in the solar system, as racist. Kweisi Mfume and his organization had some of the toughest guys in town apologizing all over the place. As my old friend John Leo, of *U.S. News & World Report*, put it, "If these people [network executives] are hard-core racists, systematically excluding blacks and other minorities in the entertainment business, we have some stop-the-press news."

But while the NAACP was busy accusing the Moguls of segregation, there was another kind of ethnic purification going on in the plastic hallways of the television business. This time, it had nothing to do with make-believe shows in Hollywood. This time, the whitewashing was going on in the sacred halls of the network news divisions in New York.

The dirty little secret is this: the top producers and executives who decide what stories get on the air don't want blacks on their prime-time news magazines any more than the Moguls in Hollywood want them in their prime-time sitcoms.

And the news elites—despite their devotion to equality and all that—don't want Hispanics on their magazine shows, either. Or poor people—no matter what color they are.

I'm not talking about the race or ethnicity of reporters. At all the networks, there's a real commitment to get black and other minority journalists on the air. This is about the real-life characters whose stories are told on shows like *48 Hours* and *Dateline* and *20/20*, the programs that, because they're much cheaper to produce than Hollywood dramas, can make the networks a lot of money if they get big enough ratings.

The line I heard over and over again at CBS News and from several sources at NBC was, "They're not our audience. They don't watch us." There was a feeling that if the characters were black or Hispanic or lower class, "our [CBS News] audience" wouldn't be able to identify with them or care about their problems, because CBS news viewers are mostly older white people who live away from the big cities.

Just like the Moguls on the West Coast, when money is on the line, when their jobs and their hefty salaries are at stake, the liberal news media do what money demands.

The problem is that, over the years, news has morphed into entertainment. To the network brass, *Dateline* is the same as *ER* or *Friends*. They all have to compete for prime-time audiences. At CBS, *48 Hours* is the same as *Everybody Loves Raymond*. At ABC, *20/20* is on the exact same prime-time schedule as *The Practice* and *Who Wants to Be a Millionaire*.

They're all shows! They all have to get good ratings to survive. News isn't special, the way it was in the early days of television. News magazines aren't on the air to perform some public service. Maybe they were when *60 Minutes* got started, but not anymore. Prime-time news magazines are on TV to make money, just like everything else on television. So they have to play by entertainment's rules.

They have to be watched by people who have money to spend on products that are advertised on those shows. So they do what the

Hollywood Moguls do. They make sure their characters appeal to their audience, which in the world of big network television means the more middle-class white people the better.

If black people were big consumers of news magazine shows, then the network producers would have some incentive to find stories about black people. But are they? Do blacks watch news magazines in big enough numbers for the mostly white producers in New York, who always have ratings on their minds, to put black people on the air?

The answer is—not really.

According to Nielsen, during that same second quarter of 1999, six of the top twenty-five shows among white viewers were news magazines. But none of those shows finished in the top twenty-five with black viewers.

Program Name	White Rank	Black Rank
60 Minutes	7	26
Dateline Monday	12	81
20/20 Wednesday	14	35
Dateline Friday	14 (tie)	85
Dateline Tuesday	14 (tie)	55
20/20 Friday	21	38

So just as the West Coast big shots don't want too many blacks as main characters on *Frasier* or *Friends*, the news Moguls don't want too many black characters in stories on *48 Hours* or *Dateline* or *20/20*—and for the exact same reason: white audiences want to see characters who look like they do. People they can identify with. Joyce Maynard, the novelist, calls it "the virtually endless fascination most of us feel for watching ourselves and our neighbors on television."

Or as a producer at *48 Hours* puts it, "All we do around here is murder, murder, murder, murder, sex. And only about white people."

That producers talk this way is only a secret to outsiders, to the civilians in the audience. At the networks, inside the news magazines, it's no secret at all. I spoke to many producers who, with only slight variations, told the same story: White characters appeal to more viewers than black characters. More viewers mean higher ratings. So we pick white characters whenever we can!

Av Westin, a producer who worked with Ed Murrow at CBS and ran *20/20* in the 1980s for ABC, did a survey (in 2000) of network journalists for the Freedom Forum and came to the same conclusion. One source told him, "We do not feature black people. I mean, it's said. Actually, they whisper it, 'Is she white?'"

Over the years, I picked up tidbits just like that from producers I worked with, stories that were told over dinner or in the car on the way to a story. I won't share their names in order to protect the innocent. Bad things happen to news people who tell stories about their own newsrooms, especially when the stories are embarrassingly true.

In 1999, I was shooting a story for *48 Hours* about kids who were in jail for serious, violent crimes, including murder. The main character in the piece was a teenage black girl. The senior staff in New York didn't know she was black but were suspicious. So one New York producer asked the field producer, "What is she?" meaning what color or ethnic group is she.

"She's black," the producer told his boss in New York, "but she's *light-skinned*." He felt he had to say that to get the okay to proceed with the story. If she were just plain old black, the New York brass might have balked and told him to find another character, meaning another character who wasn't black. He was embarrassed about the incident because he knew how it sounded.

Another *48 Hours* producer told me about a Hispanic man with a slight accent who was edited out of his story before it aired. Was the man understandable? I asked him. "Absolutely. Totally." Then why did they edit him out? "Because they don't think our audience cares about Hispanics."

This concern for race and ethnicity is common knowledge at *48 Hours*. One producer told me he would be asked, "'What racial background are these people?' They were not subtle at all. They made it pretty damn clear to me that 'we want stories with white folks.'"

"It was tough to take," he went on, and it was the "most explosive piece of inside information I was privy to."

What information exactly was that? I asked him.

"That it was racist."

Another producer, who has worked at several networks, told me that when he worked in the CBS News Dallas bureau, there was "a general understanding" that the Evening News didn't want stories about Mexicans or Indians. "Why not?" I asked him. The answer: "They think nobody cares about them."

An NBC News correspondent told me that "a white rags to riches story will make it [on a magazine program] far more quickly than a black rags to riches story." Why? "Let's not kid ourselves," he said, "these shows make a tremendous amount of money. There's no profit in people of color."

These paragons of liberalism who run the magazine shows aren't just afraid of turning off their mostly white audiences by putting minorities on the air, they're also worried about scaring their viewers with ugly people!

I have a memo entitled "*48 Hours* Survival Guide." It's an unsigned but serious three-page paper handed out to the producers on the staff, outlining what makes a good *48 Hours* story. In it, I found this gem:

"Looks count, too. This is television after all. You can find the most articulate character in the world but if she has no teeth or has a beard, no one will hear what she is saying. Therefore you must ALWAYS meet your character in person BEFORE any shoot."

Since there aren't that many toothless or bearded women out there, what the memo is really saying is: No Fat Chicks with Big Noses on *48 Hours*—presumably, even if one is a doctor who just found a cure for cancer.

We wouldn't want to frighten our viewers, now, would we?

In the spring of 2000, I launched an experiment. During the May "sweeps," one of the key months when ratings are used to determine how much the networks can charge for future commercials, I monitored all the editions of *20/20* (10 shows, 26 stories), *48 Hours* (6 shows, 12 stories), *60 Minutes* (4 shows, 12 stories), and *Dateline* (15 shows, 39 stories)—35 programs in all, 89 stories—to see if, and to what extent, the news media elites were whitewashing their magazine shows.

There were hundreds of characters in the stories, but I was only interested in the main characters, the ones the stories were about. Here's what I found:

Dateline ran stories about every titillating subject under the sun, which is what TV magazines routinely do during sweeps. They did pieces on prostitutes in Eastern Europe . . . about Rave parties where kids dance and take drugs . . . they ran "A family reunion you'll never forget" . . . they had a story about lie detectors . . . about kicking the smoking habit . . . about testosterone . . . about killer tornadoes . . . about people who survived car wrecks and fires . . . there was a story about air-conditioning units called "Silent Killer" . . . there was a piece about a nasty dog breeder . . . and, of course, there was the mandatory "murder mystery" involving the death of a little girl.

So how many blacks were featured as main characters in those fifteen *Dateline* shows that aired thirty-nine stories? A grand total of . . . *zero!* South Africa in the bad old days was more integrated than *Dateline* during sweeps!

How about *48 Hours?* There was a show called "It's Just Sex," about what Dan Rather called "The New Sexual Revolution." There was a show about doctors who take unnecessary risks with their patients. And there were plenty of murder shows: a "seventy-seven-year-old grandmother hot on the trail of a killer"... "newlyweds murdered in their small hometown"... two unsolved murders that we will "Never Forget"... and "A *48 Hours* Mystery" about a woman charged with murdering her own mother.

Blacks? None in the entire sweeps month. Not one. Same as *Dateline*.

20/20 had stories about: a serial killer...a scorned wife and the "temptress" who stole her husband... a guy who gets shot out of a cannon... a doctor who carved his initials on a patient... a rape victim trying to keep her attacker in prison... a young man charged with killing his best friend in the desert...a pedophile... an alleged thief who swindled insurance companies... and a girl who killed her mother, "a daughter's dark side."

Of the twenty-six stories *20/20* ran on ten hours' worth of shows, two of the main characters were black. One of the stories was about Secretary of Defense William Cohen and, as Barbara Walters put it, "his stunning wife Janet," who is black. As I watched I couldn't help but think that if she wasn't so stunning—which she most certainly was—*20/20* might not have found her interesting enough to put on TV during sweeps.

And then there's *60 Minutes*, the show that marches to its own drummer. *60 Minutes* was on four times during sweeps with twelve stories. Seven of them featured black people as main characters.

About five months later, in its October 2000 issue, *Brill's Content* did a story about two black producers who quit their jobs at *Dateline* because they were convinced that stories about black people were seen by network news executives as "not marketable." As part of the story, *Brill's Content* conducted the same survey as I did during the May sweeps and came up with the same numbers.

But *Brill* went a step further. Its reporter also surveyed the same news magazine shows in June, a less important month because sweeps had already ended. The author of the piece, Robert Schmidt, found an interesting difference.

Dateline, which had no blacks on in May, had three "blacks in key roles" in June, out of sixty stories.

20/20, which had two blacks on in May, had eight major black characters on in June, in forty-two stories.

48 Hours, which had no blacks on in May, had four on in June, in forty stories. And *60 Minutes*, which had seven black main characters on during sweeps, had two on in the fifteen stories it ran in June.

The *Brill's Content* piece also pointed out that over the years, "Each one [of the news magazine shows] has done solid stories on blacks or other minorities."

America is a country where race only divides, Shelby Steele wrote in *The Content of Our Character*. So maybe it's unreasonable to think that TV news executives would do better in racial matters than presidents and senators and even well-meaning, everyday Americans have been able to do in the past.

In the old days, on programs like *48 Hours*, we did dark shows on crime and punishment. And many of the characters we showed were black.

When crack was new, we showed black men selling it on street corners.

When we showed young schoolgirls having babies, many of the young schoolgirls we showed were black.

When we showed suspects being handcuffed and loaded into police cars, the ones we showed were often black.

But when we realized this emphasis on black people doing destructive things was excessive, we went to the other extreme. To atone for past sins, we tried not to show any blacks in a bad light. Such was the power of images, we believed, that showing even one black man in handcuffs would somehow slander all black men.

And when TV news magazines began to clone themselves in the 1990s, when we saw what a gold mine they were, we became very practical. We made secret, unofficial pacts—understandings, really, that didn't need to be formalized with anything more than a knowing look, if that—to marginalize blacks and other minorities and, of course, poor people, no matter what color they were.

This wasn't about sensitivity anymore, or political correctness. It wasn't about not wanting to show certain Americans in a bad light. It was about not wanting to show certain Americans at all, if we could get away with it.

Edward R. Murrow's "Harvest of Shame," the great CBS News documentary about poor migrant families traveling America, trying to survive by picking fruits and vegetables, would never be done today. Too many poor people. Not our audience. We want the people who buy cars and computers. Poor migrants won't bring our kind of Americans—the ones with money to spend—into the tent. This is how the media's "Liberals of Convenience" operate. These are the people who can spot a bigot a hundred miles away. But what they refuse to see is that they're the ones behaving just like Archie Bunker when he found out the Jeffersons were moving next door. Archie didn't really dislike black people. They just made him feel . . . *uncomfortable*. And besides, they brought property values down in the neighborhood, didn't they? What's a guy to do?

The Liberals of Convenience don't dislike blacks. Or Hispanics. Or poor people. Quite the opposite. They like them very much—*in theory*. They just don't want too many of them on their TV shows. This is what happens when entertainment and news get too chummy, when the so-called values of one become the values of the other.

This is how the game is played in the shallow money trench and the plastic hallway.

The Most Important Story You Never Saw on TV 11

I**t's true.** I *am* a Renaissance man.

For this I thank television news, because television news has kept me informed and in-the-know about all the important and significant events of our time, things that any Renaissance man must know.

For example, I know that if the glove doesn't fit, I must acquit.

I know that if you're a man, you don't want to sleep anywhere near a woman named Lorena Bobbitt, especially if you might have offended her in some way.

I know a lot about Joey Buttafuoco. In fact, I know much more about Mr. Buttafuoco than I care to know.

I know that America's delicate princess on ice skates, Tonya Harding, said it was Jeff Gillooly's idea to whack Nancy Kerrigan across the knees and that Jeff said Tonya knew a lot more than she was letting on.

Yes, I know all that and much more, thanks to television news.

I know so much about Elian Gonzalez that for weeks before it finally happened, I was rooting for the U.S. government to send him back to

Fidel Castro's communist dictatorship, just so I wouldn't have to listen to his cousin Marisleysis anymore.

And of course I know just about everything about JonBenet Ramsey, except for that pesky part about who killed her.

In fact, the reason I know that JonBenet and O.J. and Tonya and Jeff and Joey and Amy and Lorena and John and Elian and Marisleysis and Versace and Princess Di are among the most important and significant stories of our time is because TV news, according to my estimate, ran a hundred million hours of stories about them.

Back in the 1950s, Ed Murrow told us that TV could go in one of two directions: it could teach, illuminate, and even inspire us, he said, or it could be nothing more than wires and lights in a box. Let's be real generous and say the jury is still out on that one.

But while important journalists were falling all over themselves trying to land the big interview with the Ramseys or O.J.—in TV talk they call this the "get"—while Katie and Connie were sending fruit baskets and handwritten notes hoping to get the get, they all missed another pretty big story. Maybe not as big as Barbara Walters's interview with Mel Gibson, but pretty big nonetheless.

This was the story about the terrible things that are happening to America's children. The one outlined in a brilliant *Policy Review* essay entitled "Home-Alone America" by the social scientist Mary Eberstadt. Ms. Eberstadt writes, "The essence of home-alone America is just this: Over the past few decades, more and more parents have been spending less and less time at home, and most measures of what social scientists call 'child well-being' have simultaneously been in what once would have been judged scandalous decline."

Or we can put it another way: as more and more mothers have opted for work outside of the house over taking care of their children at home—and not always for economic reasons—the results have been disastrous.

While, thanks to TV news, I know all sorts of things about the afore-mentioned Joey Buttafuoco, I did not know that between 1979 and 1988 the suicide rate for girls aged ten to fourteen rose 27 percent. And for boys it went up a frightening 71 percent.

Neither did I know that between 1980 and 1997, the number of sex-ual abuse cases in America increased by 350 percent, some of the rise due to the changing mandatory reporting laws, but also, as Mary Eberstadt reports, "Here, too, a connection to home-alone America seems undeniable. For while children do risk abuse at the hands of bio-logical parents, they are *much* more likely to be abused by a cohabiting male who is not biologically related . . . [and] that in order for predatory males (and they are almost always males) to abuse, they must first have access; and that the increasing absence from home of biological moth-ers . . . effectively increases the access of would-be predators."

Thanks to TV news, I knew that John Wayne Bobbitt had surgery to attach his detached you-know-what, but I didn't know that a sociologist named Arlie Russell Hochschild discovered that "a study of nearly five thousand eighth-graders and their parents found that children who were home alone for eleven or more hours a week were three times more likely than other children to abuse alcohol, tobacco or marijuana." To which Eberstadt adds: "There is also the related question of what those hours of uninterrupted access to the violence and pornography of the Internet are doing to adolescents nationwide."

Neither did I know that, according to the National Center for Health Statistics, in 1970 fewer than 5 percent of girls under age fifteen had had sex. Today, about *one out of every three girls* that age is having sex. And I didn't know that researchers had found that some three million teenagers are affected with a sexually transmitted disease—each year.

Television news did tell me that American students don't do as well academically as kids in some other advanced countries. And I remem-ber stories about how this is probably because of economic and cultural factors. But one other possible explanation didn't get much coverage. It's the one that says while kids need help with their homework, in many American homes, nobody is there to provide that help since both mom and dad are at work.

While I knew that Korean and Japanese kids, generally speaking, score higher than American kids on standardized tests, the evening newscasts never shared with me the fact that the scholar Francis Fukuyama looked into this and concluded, "Part of the reason that children in both societies do so well on international tests has to do with the investments their mothers make in their educations."

It's not that there's been a television news blackout on all the bad things happening to our kids; we do get a story here about teen suicide and one there about test scores. It's just that the elite journalists in network television have no desire to connect the dots. They don't report the really big story—arguably one of the biggest stories of our time—that this absence of mothers from American homes is without any historical precedent, and that millions upon millions of American children have been left, as Eberstadt puts it, "to fend for themselves"—with dire consequences.

In the mid-1990s, the Census Bureau estimated that about two in ten American kids between the ages of five and fourteen—about 4.5 million of them—were "latchkey children," which is defined by the bureaucrats as those who "care for self" outside of school.

Except many of them are not caring for themselves very well. They have fallen into a kind of pit of emptiness and alienation. What's especially noteworthy is that this decline in their well-being has been happening at the same time that more and more mothers have decided to leave home for the workplace. Why has this story become such a taboo as far as the network television elites are concerned?

Why have the evening newscasts tiptoed around the most sensitive of all issues involving children—the day-care issue—going out of their way to accentuate the positive and deemphasize the negative?

"Among married women with preschool children under the age of six," the sociologist Andrew Hacker wrote in the *New York Review of Books*, "fully seven in ten now have paid employment." Not all of them work full-time and not all of them leave their children with strangers in day-care centers. Still, as Hacker tells us, this represents "a new approach to motherhood," one in which "most [women] are disinclined to make caring for their children their primary occupation."

This is a truly remarkable statement. *"Most [women] are disinclined to make caring for their children their primary occupation."* But apparently this monumental change in how we live our lives and raise our children is not nearly as monumental to TV journalists as finding out who killed JonBenet or trying to learn, as we were in much of 2001, "Where's Chandra?"

"Of all the explosive subjects in America today," Mary Eberstadt writes, "none is as cordoned off, as surrounded by rhetorical landmines, as the question of whether and just how much children need their parents—especially their mothers." The subject "is essentially off-limits for public debate," she writes.

But why? Eberstadt, being a scholar, comes up with some scholarly explanations. Partly, it's because divorce has become so commonplace in America, she says, that "a sizeable majority of Americans have tacitly, but nonetheless decidedly, placed the whole phenomenon [of kids being without their mothers at crucial times of the day] beyond public judgment."

She's probably right, but I've come up with several other reasons why this major event of our time has produced a great big yawn, at least as far as TV news is concerned.

One is that national TV reporters, as a group, are lazy. I know this is a generalization, and I know that Mark Twain said generalizations aren't worth a damn, but it's generally true nonetheless. "There's no culture of ideas around here," one CBS News executive told me, meaning hardly any of his reporters ever look out at the bigger American culture and wonder why certain things are happening and come up with something resembling an original story. These reporters and producers cover news conferences and plane crashes and hurricanes and easy stuff like that. But, despite an occasional scoop out of Washington, even this executive doesn't expect too much serious journalism out of his people, the kind that actually requires some work.

The second reason is equally "benign." Unlike O. J. and JonBenet and Chandra and the Bobbitts, stories about the loneliness and sadness of children and what happens when they don't have parents around, aren't sufficiently mysterious or sexy, two of the major ingredients that go into a good story in the often shallow world of television news. The media do get interested, of course, when one of these latchkey kids shoots up his school and kills a few students and teachers. But this interest doesn't stem from some journalistic curiosity about the empty lives of many latchkey kids—after all, most latchkey kids don't go on killing sprees. Rather, it comes from the cold fact that dead kids in the school cafeteria make for what they like to call "good TV."

The third reason is a little trickier and has to do with the similarities between network anchormen and politicians, both of whom from time to time must go to their constituents for votes in order to keep their jobs. Here's what I mean: while a congressman asks for your vote every two years, and the president every four years, and a senator every six years, anchormen ask for your vote five nights a week. As with politicians, if you don't believe they understand and sympathize with you, there's a good chance you'll vote for the other guy. If working mothers are the majority, and if they are "disinclined to make caring for their children their primary occupation," then running stories about how badly their children are doing is not going to be popular, is it? Especially given that the not-so-subtle implication is that working mothers aren't doing a very good job raising their children. That implication might first induce guilt (which probably isn't too far below the surface), but then morph into anger. That anger will be aimed squarely at the messenger, and the TV newsman or woman who delivers the story will be seen as uncaring and unsympathetic to the plight of working moms. This is not a good way to get votes, Nielsen or otherwise.

Or as Brian C. Robertson put it in his book, *There's No Place Like Work*, "A good deal of the neglect [of the troubling data on day care and latchkey kids], no doubt, derives from the reluctance ... of many academics and opinion leaders to be seen as hostile to the social advancement of women."

There is, I think, one more reason, closely tied to that fear of being seen as hostile to women-as-underdog-working-mothers. It is that the media elites will not take on feminists. Feminists are the pressure group that the media elites (and their wives and friends) are most aligned with.

Feminists tend to see any discussion that raises troubling questions about latchkey kids or younger children in day care not as an opportunity to learn and discuss something important, but as an out-and-out attack on women and the freedoms they've won since the 1970s. That fear is not completely groundless. Because it is true, as Eberstadt writes, that "Once ... staying home with one's children was judged the right thing to do, both intrinsically and for reason of the greater good, by mothers, fathers, and most of the rest of society. Today, the social expectations are exactly reversed."

But that doesn't mean that reasonable people who worry about what's happening to our children are calling for a return to the old days, when women—partly because of custom and partly because of sex discrimination—stayed home all day, preferably in the kitchen, preferably baking cookies. One can be in favor of women's advances and still be concerned about the attendant costs, especially when the costs are borne by children. If the media were open-minded, there would be a true debate about this issue. Instead, we get the usual suspects on the TV screen who call for more "quality" day care and for legislation that would give working mothers easier access to foreign nannies and for laws that would guarantee more paid maternity leave. These are all policies that would make it easier for working moms to continue working and spend *less* time with their children. Why don't we get to see intelligent voices that would reverse that equation and say that it's more important for more women to spend more time with their children and not bring in a second income?

Over the years I have seen many stories about day care, and I have come away with the impression that most mothers who work pretty much have to work in order to make ends meet. But it turns out that isn't so. Many, in fact, work outside the house because "they prefer to arrange their lives that way," as Eberstadt puts it:

> Here is where a genuine cultural revolution in motherhood can be said to have occurred. It is of course true, and has been true for all time, that significant numbers of women do leave children at home out of genuine necessity, whether for reasons of poverty, divorce, failure to marry in the first place, low educational attainment, and other familiar constraining facts of life. . . .
>
> Yet just as it is obvious that many women work because they must, it is also obvious that genuine material constraints do not begin to account for our contemporary rate of maternal absence—far from it. . . .
>
> Indeed: If the latest social science analyses prove anything, it is that more and more women are working outside the home not because they "must," but because they prefer to spend those hours there—and are increasingly inclined to acknowledge the fact. "Must" and "need," as anyone knows, are exceedingly elastic concepts where individual desires are concerned.

Robert Rector of the Heritage Foundation found that "nearly 80 percent of the preschool children using any form of day care come from married-couple families with two income earners." I don't remember ever hearing that on the network news. Katha Pollitt, the feminist, has written, "The truth is, the day-care debate has always been about college-educated working moms." I don't remember hearing that either on the nightly newscasts. But it makes sense. As anyone who lives in a middle-class neighborhood anywhere in this country knows, a lot of people think they "must" work outside the house because they "need" a certain six-figure lifestyle, or, for the sake of their sanity, they "need" to be around grown-ups doing some kind of work that is more creative than changing diapers and talking baby talk.

That is for them to decide. Every year or so we seem to get another study on day care—this one saying it's good for kids, the next one saying it's not so good. I'm confused and my guess is that not too many adults go into therapy because their mother dropped them off at day care when they were four years old. But in any case, this is not an argument for or against mothers leaving the house to work in an office or a factory. That is not my concern, despite the troubling statistics, at least relating to latchkey children.

The argument here is that once again the elite journalists on television have taken sides. Too many day-care centers in America are not as good as they ought to be, they and their "experts" frequently tell us, so the challenge is to spend more government money to subsidize day care and to make it better. I am not against "better day care," and I have no problem with the evening news doing stories about how that might be done. The problem is that they don't let the other voices on. The ones who say that most toddlers are better off with their own mothers than with day-care workers and that most adolescent kids would do better if a parent were home after school instead of being alone and "fending for themselves."

In May 2001, Rich Lowry offended feminists from Maine to California when he wrote in the conservative *National Review*, "Work has, in post-feminist America, become central to the identity of women (and child-rearing doesn't count). Work is an act of historical redemption for all those centuries of oppression and sexism, so that sounding at all skeptical about it is to be identified with those former forces of darkness. When negative day-care studies appear, there's a palpable worry, not that the children are endangered, but that women's careers are."

He was writing in response to a government study on day care that came out in April 2001, and concluded that toddlers who are put in day care for long stretches of time tended to be more aggressive and defiant, *regardless of the quality of the day care.* The study was done by the National Institute of Child Health and Human Development and says that 17 percent of kids who are left in day-care centers for more than thirty hours a week argue a lot, demand a lot of attention, act cruelly, show explosive behavior, talk too much, and get into lots of fights.

So would Tom and Peter and Dan use this study to launch a serious discussion about whether some kids might be better off with mom at home? Or about whether dads should be paid a "family wage"? Or about how this report is a vindication for stay-at-home moms?

No.

On CBS, Dan Rather called the study "controversial"—twice. This seems like a good time to point out that whenever you hear an anchorman or reporter use the word "controversial," it is usually a signal that the idea that follows is one the media elites do not agree with.

But why would a study that concludes what sounds like plain old common sense—that some very young children behave aggressively when they're away from their mothers for long stretches of time—be considered *controversial?* Because such a conclusion is guaranteed to make many of those working mothers—especially the better educated ones from two-hefty-income households—feel guilty. And this is something the anchor-politicians cannot do for fear of looking unsympathetic and losing their Nielsen vote. Which is why such a study's findings are described as "controversial."

This is how Dan opened his evening newscast that night in April: "A controversial call to working parents: A new study claims child day-care often leads to behavior nightmares." Then a few seconds later: "Good evening. The millions of parents who dropped their children off at day care this morning have something important to think about tonight: A new study that makes controversial claims about the impact of day care."

On NBC, Robert Hager also found the study "controversial." On the *Nightly News* he reported, "Today a controversial new report claims a downside, says preschoolers sent to day care become somewhat more aggressive than others, experience more behavioral problems by the time they get to kindergarten."

Two days after the report came out, on CBS's *Saturday Early Show*, we got another "controversial" take on the study. Co-host Russ Mitchell, introducing the story, said, "CBS News correspondent Cynthia Bowers has more on these controversial findings that are bound to worry working parents."

Russ was absolutely right: the conclusion that some kids behave badly when they spend long hours in day care would surely worry working parents. But what Russ left out was that many of those working parents were working right there alongside him in the newsroom. Let's remember that while Russ Mitchell and Dan Rather and Robert Hager aren't working mothers, they work with a lot of women who are, and as Dan might put it, *those gals got a dog in this fight.* America's newsrooms are filled with women who drop their kids off someplace before they go to work or leave them at home with the nanny. These journalists are not just defending working mothers—*they're defending themselves!*

And it's not just working *moms.* Many of those supposedly objective journalist *dads* who write about day-care studies also have a dog in the fight. Many of them want their wives to work. Like many media elites, these people would rather swallow shards of glass than vacation with "red state" Americans in a place like, say, Branson, Missouri, one of the most popular tourist spots in the entire United States. So if they encourage, or perhaps even insist, that their wives leave little Adam or Nicole at home with a nanny or at day care with some "caregiver," and she goes to work and earns a second paycheck, then they can take a nice vacation—not in the Ozarks—but maybe in Paris. And they can also live in a bigger house and drive something a little fancier than a Chevy or a Ford.

The feminist response to any "controversial" news about day care is to call for more federal laws and subsidies to improve the quality of day care. Which is why Dan invited the president of the Children's Defense Fund, Marian Wright Edelman, on his evening newscast the night the study came out to tell the audience that the answer to the day-care problem was—surprise!—more federal laws and subsidies for better day care. The federal government, Ms. Edelman said, should "put into place the kind of quality, comprehensive system and sets of choices that many other industrialized countries have." In other words, if it's good enough for Sweden, it ought to be good enough for the United States.

Over at ABC, Peter Jennings was thinking the same thing. After a news report on the day-care study, Peter offered up some thoughts. "Federal law," he said, "only requires companies with fifty or more workers to give new mothers twelve weeks' leave—and without pay, at that. The U.S. is actually the least generous of the industrialized nations. In Sweden, a new mother gets eighteen months of maternity and parental leave, and she gets 80 percent of her salary for the first year. Mother or father can take the parental leave any time until a child is eight. England gives eighteen weeks' maternity leave. For the first six weeks, a mother gets 90 percent of her salary from the government and $86 a week thereafter. German women get two months of fully paid leave after giving birth. The government and the company kick in. And either parent has the option of three full years in parental leave with some of their salary paid and their jobs protected. And finally, in Canada, new parents can take up to a year of leave. Depending on how much they make, they get from 55 to 80 percent of [their] salaries."

Forget for a moment that Peter was sounding like he was delivering a not-so-stealthy editorial for laws to make it easier for parents to leave their kids in day care. That aside, aren't there any voices we might hear from the other side, from all those women who would rather *not* work outside the home, who would rather spend *more* time with their children, and who would like to see their political leaders fight for tax *cuts* so that they could work *less* and not have to drop the kids off at day care or leave them home alone after school?

In fact, this is *exactly* what Steve Forbes said when he was running for president in 1996 and arguing that his flat tax would give parents "more time to spend with their children and with each other." But no one brought Forbes on as another intelligent voice to go along with Marian Wright Edelman. *No one at CBS News thought the issue was worth debating. The "controversial" study merely needed to be "corrected" by Edelman.*

Why is one point of view valid and the other nonexistent on the evening news? Maybe because a few years earlier the same CBS News mocked the very idea that Forbes put forth in his presidential campaign, with the CBS News correspondent characterizing it as "Forbes's number one wackiest flat tax promise."

On network TV, given the prevailing sensibilities that reign there, voices that argue for policies that would make it easier for moms to drop their kids off at day care are considered thoughtful, compassionate, and reasonable. But voices that argue for *less* day care, because day care is bad for kids—frankly, I don't think the media elites *even know such voices exist.*

In his *National Review* piece, Rich Lowry writes that there is a tendency "in academia and the media to find a way to pronounce anything associated with day care—*up to and including infectious illness*...a good thing, so as to shield working mothers from any bad news." [Emphasis added.]

He's not kidding. Even germs are turned into good news when it comes to day care. Lowry was referring to research done by David Murray of the Statistical Assessment Service in Washington, D.C. A study in the *New England Journal of Medicine* in August 2000 found that kids who attended day care in their first six months were less likely to have asthma at age thirteen. The theory was that by being exposed to so many germs and infections so early, the kids developed resistance.

The big-time media loved the story. The *Boston Globe* announced, "Day Care May Gird Children Against Asthma." The headline in the *Washington Post* said, "Day Care May Boost Immunity to Asthma; Early Exposure to Germs Is Cited." The *New York Times* ran this gleeful headline: "Day Care, for Keeping Asthma at Bay."

CNN ran a big story, complete with an "on camera" ending in which the reporter, Christy Feig, passed along the good news: "Parents who may worry about their children getting sick from other children can now relax a little. It may benefit them down the road."

But Murray points out an inconvenient fact that might have toned down those headlines.

"The dramatic rise in the number of children attending early day care," he writes, "exactly coincides with the epidemic rise of childhood asthma.... Childhood asthma more than doubled between 1980 and the present [October 2000], just as did the pattern of working parents choosing early day care. Hence, positing a cause and effect relationship between day care and reduced asthma faces a formidable hurdle."

Still, despite the questionable evidence that day care really does keep asthma at bay, CNN and the big newspapers loved the story precisely, one could argue, because it was "good" news about day care. But now look at how the media handled another study about germs and infectious diseases involving children and day care—this one not so good news.

In October 1999, the *Journal of the American Medical Association* analyzed hospitalizations due to respiratory infections among American kids between 1980 and 1996. Murray writes, "The study examined respiratory syncytial virus (RSV), which causes more lower respiratory tract infections among young children than any other pathogen. They found that the rate had increased substantially, and argued that the true scope of the problem had been previously underestimated."

David Murray then writes that the "associated factors were multiple, but quite prominently mentioned was the effect of day care. As the study notes, 'Attendance at a child-care center with six or more other children is an independent risk factor for [a] lower respiratory tract disease hospitalization in the first two years of life. . . . A trend toward earlier enrollment in large child-care centers may lead to initial RSV infection at a younger age, when hospitalization is more likely. Specifically child-care practices must be examined in relation to bronchiolitis hospitalization trends.'"

"The research," Murray concludes, "appearing in a major medical journal, offered a clear warning sign about the consequences of emerging social practices [putting young children in large day-care centers]."

So how did the media play this one?

They didn't. Murray says, "The press reaction was strangely muted. A Lexis-Nexis search found only a 450-word Associated Press synopsis . . . but the wire story was picked up by no newspaper. . . . The stark fact is that news accounts of any research positing a negative health outcome attributed to day care are few and far between."

I ran a Lexis-Nexis search, too, and found only two very brief mentions on network television: fifty-one words on the *CBS Morning Show* and seventy-three words on the *Today* show. Both were items read by the news anchors. Neither CBS nor NBC sent a reporter out to actually cover the story. And I could find nothing on any of the evening newscasts.

Maybe the media elites are right not to throw this kind of bad news in the face of working moms, who feel bad enough as it is, even though some of them obviously would feel worse if they had to stay at home with their kids. "Career moms," Rich Lowry says, "need such coddling for a reason. Mothers who choose to work full-time jobs and routinely leave their young children with others for much of the day are not normal: They are a historical aberration; they represent a minority preference among women; and they run exactly counter to the standard of motherhood that should be encouraged by society. No wonder elite culture treats them as hothouse flowers, who must hear nary a discouraging word. But the fact is that working moms are at the very center of a variety of cultural ills. Maybe a little stigma is what they deserve.

"We are willing to do anything 'for the children,'" Lowry says, "except suggest that their mothers should stay with them; we are committed to 'leaving no child behind' unless it is by his mother hustling off to make her career."

You won't hear that voice on the evening news, either.

And because we don't hear that voice on the evening news, television news has kept its viewers ignorant of one of the biggest and most important social changes of our times.

Marjorie Williams of the *Washington Post* gave voice to media elite opinion when she wrote that she lives "with the knowledge that in pursuing my work, I am to some degree acting selfishly." But at the same time, she hopes she will eventually be able to explain to her five-year-old that "what I do at that desk [at the newspaper] feels as necessary to me as food or air." To which Mary Eberstadt adds: "These are evocative words in more ways than one. They are the sort of things mothers have also said about their children."

Liberal Hate-Speech 12

If arrogance were a crime, there wouldn't be enough jail cells in the entire United States to hold all the people in TV news.

A network correspondent told me that once, but when he found out I was writing a book he got amnesia. Not only couldn't he remember ever saying such a subversive thing, but if by some insane chance he had—which he hadn't, of course—he didn't want any credit for it.

No problem.

Except that when network news correspondents are afraid to say even something as harmless as that out loud, there's not much chance they'll take on more serious problems, which then leaves the field wide open to idiots like me or, more ominously, to the real pros . . . the conservative media watchdogs that monitor every second of network news in order to document every single example of liberal bias, real or imagined.

Such an organization is the Media Research Center, based in Alexandria, Virginia, right outside Washington, D.C. Every month or so MRC mails a newsletter to reporters and anchors and other sages in the big-time national media. "Notable Quotables," they call it, is chock-full of "the latest outrageous, sometimes humorous, quotes in the liberal media." They also put out a daily report online called CyberAlert, which MRC says tracks media bias.

You'd think this exposure, before your own colleagues no less, might cause a certain amount of embarrassment, especially when the example of bias is especially egregious. Dream on. Network correspondents don't embarrass easily.

It's easy to dismiss "Notable Quotables," because professional liberal bashers compile it. But the right-wing scoundrels at the Media Research Center have come up with some good stuff. What follows are some of the more noteworthy examples, from the last ten years or so, of how journalists on the Left see the world.

■ "Some thoughts on those angry voters. Ask parents of any two-year-old and they can tell you about those temper tantrums: the stomping feet, the rolling eyes, the screaming. . . . Imagine a nation full of uncontrolled two-year-old rage. The voters had a temper tantrum last week. . . . Parenting and governing don't have to be dirty words: the nation can't be run by an angry two-year-old."

—ABC anchorman Peter Jennings in his radio commentary after the GOP won the House, November 14, 1994

■ "It's short of soap, so there are lice in the hospitals. It's short of pantyhose, women's legs go bare. It's short of snowsuits, so babies stay home in the winter. Sometimes it's short of cigarettes so millions of people stop smoking, involuntarily. It drives everybody crazy. The problem isn't communism; no one even talked about communism this week. The problem is shortages."

—NBC Nightly News commentator John Chancellor on the Soviet Union, August 21, 1991

■ "I would be happy to give him [Clinton] a blow job just to thank him for keeping abortion legal. I think American women should be lining up with their presidential kneepads on to show their gratitude for keeping the theocracy off our backs."

—Time *contributor and former reporter Nina Burleigh recalling what she told the* Washington Post's *Howard Kurtz about her feeling toward Bill Clinton, as recounted by Burleigh in the July 20, 1998,* New York Observer

■ "The man is on the Court. You know, I hope his wife feeds him lots of eggs and butter and he dies early like many black men do, of heart disease. Well, that's how I feel. He is an absolutely reprehensible person."

—USA Today *columnist and Pacifica Radio talk show host Julianne Malveaux on Justice Clarence Thomas, November 4, 1994, PBS,* To the Contrary

■ *Inside Washington* (TV) host Tina Gulland: "I don't think I have any Jesse Helms defenders here, Nina?"

Nina Totenberg: "Not me. I think he ought to be worried about what's going on in the Good Lord's mind, because if there is retributive justice, he'll get AIDS from a transfusion, or one of his grandchildren will get it."

—*National Public Radio and ABC News reporter Nina Totenberg reacting to Senator Jesse Helms's claim that the government spends too much on AIDS research, July 8, 1995*

■ "Yes, the case is being fomented by right-wing nuts and yes, she is not a very credible witness, and it's really not a law case at all. But Clinton has got a problem here. He has a history of womanizing that most people believe is a problem. . . . It leads to things like this, some sleazy woman with big hair coming out of the trailer parks."

—Newsweek *Washington bureau chief Evan Thomas on Paula Jones, May 7, 1994,* Inside Washington

■ "In the plague years of the 1980s—that low decade of denial, indifference, hostility, opportunism, and idiocy—government fiddled and medicine diddled and the media were silent or hysterical. A gerontocratic Ronald Reagan took this [AIDS] plague less seriously than Gerald Ford had taken swine flu. After all, he didn't need the ghettos and he didn't want the gays."

—CBS Sunday Morning *TV critic John Leonard, September 5, 1993*

■ "... Toni Morrison wrote in the *New Yorker* that Clinton was our first 'black President,' and I think, in a way, Clinton may be our first 'woman President.' And I think that may be one of the reasons why women identify, because he does have a lot of feminine qualities about him: The softness, the sensitivity, the vulnerability, that kind of thing."

—*the* Washington Post*'s Sally Quinn on* CNN*'s* Larry King Live, *March 10, 1999*

■ "He [Ted Kaczynski] wasn't a hypocrite. He lived as he wrote. His manifesto, and there are a lot of things in it that I would agree with and a lot of other people would, that industrialization and pollution are terrible things, but he carried it to an extreme, and obviously murder is something that is far beyond any political philosophy, but he had a bike. He didn't have any plumbing, he didn't have any electricity."

—Time *Washington reporter Elaine Shannon talking about the Unabomber, April 7, 1996,* Sunday Journal

■ "I think liberalism lives—the notion that we don't have to stay where we are as a society, we have promises to keep, and it is liberalism, whether people like it or not, which has animated all the years of my life. What on earth did conservatism accomplish for our country?"

—Charles Kuralt talking with Morley Safer on the CBS special
One for the Road with Charles Kuralt, *May 4, 1994*

■ Linda Chavez, Center for Equal Opportunity: "If you're someone like me, who lives out in a rural area—if someone breaks into my house and wants to murder or rape me or steal off of my property, it'll take half an hour for a policeman to get to me.... Thousands of lives are saved by people being able to protect themselves."
Bonnie Erbe, host and former NBC Radio/Mutual reporter: "And if you look at the statistics, I would bet that you have a greater chance of being struck by lightning, Linda, than living where you live, and at your age, being raped. Sorry."

—PBS, To the Contrary, *May 13, 2000*

■ "I'm all news all the time. Full power, tall tower. I want to break in when news breaks out. That's my agenda. Now respectfully, when you start talking about a liberal agenda and all the, quote, 'liberal bias' in the media, I quite frankly, and I say this respectfully but candidly to you, I don't know what you're talking about."

—Dan Rather to Denver KOA Radio's Mike Rosen,
November 28, 1995

In fairness to the media elites, these aren't really examples of *unethical* liberal bias. Dan Rather was giving his opinion on a radio talk show. Peter Jennings didn't liken the American voter to an angry two-year-old on the *World News Tonight*. He did it in a radio commentary, a place he's allowed to give his opinions. John Chancellor wasn't *reporting* the news when he made his absurd observation that the problem in the old Soviet Union wasn't communism, but shortages. He was doing *commentary*.

Liberals have as much right to be downright silly as anyone else. But I doubt Peter would have gone on a rant if liberal Democrats had been swept into office instead of conservative Republicans. I doubt he would have compared Americans voters to a bunch of babies having temper tantrums had they voted for people more to Peter's liking and the liking of his Manhattan pals.

But there is something interesting about how liberals in the media can get away with making certain observations that conservatives never could.

Nina Totenberg says, "[I]f there's retributive justice, he'll [Jesse Helms] get AIDS from a transfusion, or one of his grandchildren will get it," and she remains a member in good standing of the liberal media elites.

What if a conservative journalist such as Fred Barnes of the *Weekly Standard* had said, *"If there's any justice in this world, Teddy Kennedy will drive off a bridge late at night and kill himself. Or one or two of his kids."*

He would rightly be considered a contemptible hatemonger whose every word on every subsequent subject would be scrutinized for traces of venom, and it wouldn't be long before other journalists would marginalize him.

USA Today columnist Julianne Malveaux says of Clarence Thomas, "I hope his wife feeds him lots of eggs and butter and he dies early like many black men do, of heart disease," and she gets invited back on TV talk shows all the time.

If Robert Novak, the conservative columnist and CNN commentator, had said, *"I hope Jesse Jackson's wife feeds him lots of eggs and butter and he dies early like many black men do, of heart disease,"* he'd rightly be seen as a nasty right-wing nut and compared to the Grand Wizard of the KKK.

Newsweek's Evan Thomas cavalierly calls Paula Jones "some sleazy woman with big hair coming out of the trailer parks," and he's seen as a pundit instead of a liberal elitist snob.

Can anyone in his right mind really imagine a conservative journalist of Evan Thomas's stature ridiculing a not-too-sophisticated, not-too-educated, young black or Hispanic woman, as someone *"with big hair coming out of the ghetto"?*

Bonnie Erbe tells Linda Chavez on PBS that she's got a greater chance of being struck by lightning than being raped—*at her age.*

If Brit Hume had said something so incredibly insensitive and so downright stupid (which I know he never would), NOW would have screamed that, like so many men, he just doesn't get it, that rape is *not* about sex, but about *power and control*, and then, just to set an example, the president of NOW would have led a contingent to hang Brit Hume in effigy, or maybe in the flesh. They would have thrown a million pickets into the crusade to get him off the air, and they'd all be marching around Fox headquarters in New York and Washington chanting "Brit's a Twit and He's Got to Go." Quicker than you can say "male chauvinist pig" Brit Hume would become an embarrassment to Fox and a pariah in the world of big-time journalism.

But when a liberal says it on PBS, no big deal. Chavez is a conservative after all—and the sin of all sins, she says things Hispanic women aren't supposed to say. White liberals hate it when minorities do that. So, ipso facto, she's fair game.

Why is it that when liberal media stars say nasty things they're merely sharing their thoughts with us and (even more important) their feelings, but when the same sentiment comes out of a conservative's mouth, it's seen as mean-spirited?

After Bill Clinton was impeached, *Newsweek*'s Eleanor Clift ("Eleanor Rodham Clift," in some circles) said, "That herd of managers from the House, I mean, frankly, all they were missing was white sheets."

Likewise, the *Arkansas Times* editorialized that "Kenneth Starr is cunning, ruthless, and about as well-mannered as Heinrich Himmler."

On January 15, 1999—Martin Luther King's birthday—the *Los Angeles Times* published an op-ed by "frequent contributor" Karen Grigsby Bates who spewed the following:

"It is a totally visceral reaction, but whenever I hear [Republican Senate majority leader] Trent Lott speak, I immediately think of nooses decorating trees. Big trees, with black bodies swinging from the business end of the nooses."

This is vile. Maybe it went over big with what they like to call "the creative community" in Los Angeles, but it is vile hate speech no matter how you cut it.

And what of the *Los Angeles Times*, the newspaper that published it? The *Times* is nothing if not a monument to political correctness, so much so that an op-ed page editor yanked a line from a syndicated George Will column that said, "I think it is reasonable to believe that [Bill Clinton] was a rapist." This offended the sensibilities of the *Times* editor. Linking a United States senator to the likes of Ku Klux Klan murderers, however, apparently falls into the category of nothing to get worked up over.

The media elites, at the *Los Angeles Times* and everyplace else, can hear even the whispers of what they consider hate speech fifty miles away—whether they imagine that it's coming from conservative talk show hosts or right-wing religious fundamentalists or just about anyone opposed to affirmative action. But they can't hear it dripping off their own nasty tongues...and probably think "liberal hate-speech" is an oxymoron.

It's a good thing arrogance isn't a crime.

"The Ship Be Sinking" 13

Back in 1982, when a reporter asked New York Knicks guard Micheal Ray Richardson what the problem was with his last-place team, he offered up a succinct analysis. It consisted of just four simple words, but in the world of sport it has been enshrined.

"The ship be sinking," Micheal Ray said, rivaling "To be or not to be" for sheer elegance and beating it by two words for utter succinctness. And that would have been the end of it, except that another reporter asked a follow-up question.

"How far can it sink?"

Micheal (that's how he spells his name) considered the question, then put forth another four-word masterpiece.

"The sky's the limit."

Move over, Mr. Shakespeare, there is a new Bard in our midst.

These days another ship is taking on water. The network news divisions' own flagship: their evening newscasts.

To assess the damage, just look at the scoreboard—the Nielsen ratings.

In the 1979–80 season, 75 percent of all TV sets that were on in the early evening were tuned to a network news program, either ABC, CBS, or NBC.

Seventy-five percent!

But twenty-one years later, in 2001, the share of the audience watching network news had sunk all the way to 43 percent.

If the networks were selling shoes instead of news, they'd be out of business by now.

How far can the evening news ratings sink? Looks like the sky's the limit. The numbers get worse every year. In the 1994–95 season, for example, 51 percent of Americans with TV sets on were watching Dan or Peter or Tom. In 1995–96 it was 50 percent. For 1996–97 and 1997–98, it was 49 percent. Then it slipped to 47 percent; by the end of 2000, it was 44 percent; and in July 2001, 43 percent.

When Walter Cronkite handed Dan Rather the baton in spring 1981, the *CBS Evening News* was in first place. Twenty years later, CBS was in last place, having lost more than half its ratings.

The ABC and NBC nightly newscasts, during the same period, didn't do as badly, but their ratings plummeted, too.

With each passing year, the national evening newscast, as an American institution, is becoming less and less relevant. But that's not entirely the fault of the evening stars. Not by a long shot. Over the years, an inconvenient reality cropped up that Dan and Tom and Peter had nothing to do with and had no power to stop. Today, there are cable and satellite TV and the Internet, competition that Cronkite and Huntley and Brinkley didn't even have to think about.

It's as if the Berlin Wall had come down. But instead of voting with their feet, Americans began voting with their remote control devices. They haven't abandoned the news. Just the news people they no longer trust.

How else can we account for Bill O'Reilly and *The O'Reilly Factor* on the Fox News Channel. O'Reilly is currently the hottest anchor on the hottest news and information program on cable television.

The *Washington Post* did a profile and said O'Reilly was "cable TV's ascendant talk star."

Newsweek did a big spread—the "Life of O'Reilly," they called it— that says he makes more than a million dollars a year and has "the highest-rated cable-news program on TV."

He wrote a book, *The O'Reilly Factor*, that was a *New York Times* number-one bestseller for ten weeks.

And as far as I'm concerned, the three people Bill owes so much of his success to are Tom Brokaw, Peter Jennings, and Dan Rather.

People will get their news from the people they like and believe, which is very bad news for the old guard.

Consider a poll (of 822 randomly selected Americans) conducted by *Brill's Content* and published in its March 2000 issue.

Seventy-four percent of Republicans believe that most journalists are more liberal than they are. No bulletin, there. You'd expect Republicans to think that way.

But, as the magazine puts it, "Perhaps more surprising, Democrats also perceive a liberal media tilt: 47 percent believe that most journalists are more liberal than they are...."

Here's where the bad news comes in for Rather, Jennings, and Brokaw.

The poll finds what seems to be at least a circumstantial link between viewers' noticing "a liberal media tilt" and their defection to cable.

"And just as their overall broadcast entertainment ratings have dropped, broadcast-television network newscasts are losing to cable channels, especially those cable channels with name brands in particular news categories."

I spoke to Bill O'Reilly about this just before Christmas 2000, and he told me his viewers "perceive Rather and those guys as being left, but even more, they see them as being elitist, as not being in touch with them."

Of course, there's a good chance that a lot of the defectors from ABC, CBS, and NBC nightly news are going to O'Reilly because, no matter what they say about wanting a fair, down-the-middle newscast, what they really want is a program with a conservative tilt. I'm sure that a lot of O'Reilly's fans are right of center, that some are angry white males and females, live in the red states, and voted for George W. Bush. No one is confusing Bill O'Reilly with Bill Moyers, or Fox with PBS.

But whenever I tune in to *The O'Reilly Factor*, I hear opinions and arguments about the news of the day coming from the right and from the left. And this, I think, is what throws the critics of O'Reilly and Fox. They're just not used to hearing so many diverse views on TV, most of them fairly intelligent.

This is how Roger Ailes, O'Reilly's boss at Fox News, explained it in a *New York Times Magazine* piece in June 2001: "There are more conservatives *on* Fox. But we are *not* a conservative network. That disparity says far more about the competition." In other words, if Fox is alleged to have a conservative bias, that's only because there are so few conservative voices on the air at ABC, CBS, NBC, CNN, and MSNBC. Roger definitely is on to something, but so are the critics. There certainly *is* a conservative "attitude" at Fox, a conservative sensibility. Why else would so many conservatives be watching shows like *The O'Reilly Factor*?

When I spoke to Bill, he pointed to a favorite Ailes example of how ABC, NBC, CBS, and CNN frame the debate on a big issue like abortion. "They exclude voices in America like crazy," he told me. "You don't see an articulate spokesman who's pro-life on the network evening newscasts. They'd rather show someone who just shot up an abortion clinic."

So how does Bill O'Reilly, the man *Newsweek* calls the "Fox News phenom," assess the future of Messrs. Rather, Brokaw, and Jennings?

"It's like the last days of Pompeii. They're desperately trying to hold on. They see the smoke."

Or to put it another way: the ship be sinking.

Right after my op-ed came out, Mike Wallace was asked by a freelance reporter in Washington, "What is your reaction to CBS News reporter Bernard Goldberg's charges of liberal bias in the media?"

Mike replied, "When people suggest there is a bias in the media and we have all this power and then of course the bias is always supposed to be liberal and not conservative, well then, under those circumstances how many Democratic presidents and how many Republican presidents have there been beginning with Richard Nixon and Ronald Reagan twice, George Bush. It's just in my estimation, it's almost a joke."

I think Mike Wallace is great, but in this case the joke's on him.

Just because Americans, starting in 1980, elected Republicans president four times (Reagan twice, Bush and Bush) and Democrats only two times (Clinton twice) doesn't prove, as Mike seems to think, that there's no liberal bias. A more likely explanation is that TV news viewers simply aren't influenced by the bias they're being fed from network anchors and reporters whom they lost trust in a long time ago.

Besides, the problem of bias is not that the big network news divisions are reliably pro-Democratic . . . or even predictably anti-Republican. It's about how they frame the big issues of the day—feminism, abortion, race, affirmative action, even taxes. On these issues they are reliably and predictably left of center.

John Leo captured it in a 1997 column:

> Having worked in many newsrooms, I can tell you that most reporters are honest and try hard to be fair, but they are keenly aware of the conventional narrative line on most controversial and recurring stories. They know how such stories

are expected to be handled and how newsroom rewards and punishments tend to follow certain kinds of treatment. In his 1990 *Los Angeles Times* stories on abortion coverage, David Shaw explained how reporters could expect a challenge from colleagues when they tapped out a story that gave even indirect aid and comfort to anti-abortion forces.

Angry white male stories tend to attribute any opposition to affirmative action to social intolerance, backlash, and personal fears. Here's the opening section of a segment last year on NBC's *Dateline* dealing with two academics who got California's Proposition 209 on the ballot: "Do you feel that everyone is after your job . . . that people can criticize you and it's OK? Are you a white American male . . . the beleaguered species?" Intended to be jaunty and cute, the opening was simply snide. All it really showed is that the people at *Dateline* had difficulty imagining any principled opposition to race and gender preferences, possibly because such opposition is unknown on the *Dateline* staff.

John Leo and I have talked many times about the nature of bias in the newsroom, about how it is not some sinister plot, but about how mostly liberal journalists tend to frame stories from a mostly liberal point of view.

In my experience, I've noticed that liberals often see America as a dark place populated by all sorts of bigots who can't wait to bash one minority or another. They see America as more antigay than it is, and more racist than it is. They see America as "slouching towards Gomorrah," but not the way conservatives see it.

The view from the Right is that America has become too uncivil and too vulgar. Conservatives believe that over the years, as America became more tolerant, it became *indiscriminately* tolerant. Accepting minorities is progress. Accepting dopey sex jokes on TV sitcoms at eight o'clock at night is not progress.

From the Left, incivility and vulgarity are in the eyes of the beholder. And besides, they say, it's a sign that we've become more open and honest about things. They point to the fact that Lucy and Ricky slept in separate beds and couldn't even use the word "pregnant" on their TV show. "Is that what we want?" they ask, implying that anyone who thinks things have gone too far in the direction of Howard Stern is some sort of prude.

The real menace, as the Left sees it, is that America has always been too willing to step on its most vulnerable—gays, women, blacks. Because the Left controls America's newsrooms, we get a view of America that reflects that sensibility.

This is how John Leo put it in his column: "Polls show a large majority [of Americans] have reservations and conflicted feelings . . . when it comes to gay marriage and any teaching in the schools that amounts to an endorsement of homosexuality. In the newsroom, of course, all this is viewed as nonsense and homophobia. The upshot is that because of newsroom framing, the real national conversation on homosexuality is not really being reported. It is off the table because of the narrow view of the story in terms of prejudice."

It's the same when it comes to race.

"Journalists tend to feel that bigotry is widespread in America and they are primed to see it quickly when their counterparts in the lobbying world send in their reports. This explains why stories about alleged racial slurs among Texaco executives and the wave of church burnings in the South were still being framed as bias news long after the evidence showed that this framing was wrong. This media tilt has the effect of discounting the real gains of out-groups and depicting the country as much more prejudiced than it really is. . . . It's one reason why so few people trust the press."

And it's why the ship be sinking.

Connecting the Dots... to Terrorism 14

Most of the time television is nothing more than a diversion—proof, as the old quip goes, that we would rather do anything than talk to each other. We'd also rather watch a bad sitcom than read a good book. Bad sitcoms get millions of viewers; good books get thousands. In an "entertainment culture," even the news is entertainment. Certainly too much local news has been pure fluff for some time now, with their Ken and Barbie anchors who have nothing intelligent to say but look great while they're saying it. And because network news is losing viewers every year, executives and producers are trying to figure out ways to hold on to the ones they still have. They think cosmetics will work, so they change the anchor desk or they change the graphics. They get the anchor to stand instead of sit. They feature more "news you can use." They put Chandra Levy on all over the place, hoping they can concoct a ratings cocktail by mixing one part missing intern with ten parts sex scandal.

And then something genuinely big and really important happens that shakes us to our core, and all those producers who couldn't get enough of Chandra are through with her. Only in the fickle world of television news can someone who has disappeared without a trace disappear a second time.

And it's when that history-making story comes along that Americans—no matter what their politics, religion, age, race, or sex—turn to television, not just for information, but also for comfort and for peace of mind. It doesn't happen often, but when it does, television becomes a lot more than just a diversion.

It happened when John Kennedy was assassinated. We all turned to Walter Cronkite and Huntley and Brinkley, not just for facts, but also for reassurance—that despite the terrible tragedy, America was going to be okay.

It happened when *Challenger* blew up. And it happened again on September 11, 2001, when a band of religious lunatics declared war on the United States of America to punish us for not wanting to dwell in the fourteenth century, where they currently reside, and, of course, to show the world that their intense hatred of Israel—*and of Israel's friends*—knows no bounds. On September 11, they not only killed as many innocent Americans as they could in the most dramatic way they knew how, but, as the *Wall Street Journal* put it, they also "wiped out any remaining illusions that America is safe from mass organized violence."

On that day we all turned to television. We turned to Dan Rather and Peter Jennings and Tom Brokaw and the others. And they did a fine job, as they often do when covering tragedy. They showed empathy. They were fair and accurate, and the information they passed along to us wasn't filtered through the usual liberal political and social sensibilities. They gave us the news on that day the way they should give us the news *all the time*, whether the story is about race or feminism or taxes or gay rights or anything else. *For a change, they gave it to us straight.*

On the night of September 11, 2001, Peter Jennings made a point about how, in times of danger and tragedy, television serves the function that campfires used to serve in the old days when Americans migrated westward in covered wagons. Back then, they would sit around the campfire and get the news from other travelers about what they should look out for down the road. "Some people pulled the wagons around," Peter said, "and discussed what was going on and tried to understand it." But the campfire was more than just a meeting place where families could pick up important information. The campfire also provided a sense of community, a sense that *we're all in this together*. That's what television was on September 11.

As I listened to Peter tell that story, I thought about another American tragedy that shocked us six years earlier, when Timothy McVeigh—another true believer who cared nothing about killing innocent Americans—blew up the federal building in Oklahoma City. I thought about how it took some of the media elites only a few days before they started to play one of their favorite games—connect the dots. What they found back then—or more accurately, what they convinced themselves they found—was a line stretching from Oklahoma City to the Republican Party to conservatives in general and finally to Rush Limbaugh.

Dan Rather said, "Even after Oklahoma City, you can turn on your radio in any city and still dial up hate talk: extremist, racist, and violent from the hosts and those who call in."

Time senior writer Richard Lacayo put it this way: "In a nation that has entertained and appalled itself for years with hot talk on radio and the campaign trail, the inflamed rhetoric of the '90s is suddenly an unindicted coconspirator in the blast."

Nina Easton wrote in the *Los Angeles Times*, "The Oklahoma City attack on federal workers and their children also alters the once-easy dynamic between charismatic talk show host and adoring audience.

Hosts who routinely espouse the same antigovernment themes as the militia movement now must walk a fine line between inspiring their audience—and inciting the most radical among them."

On *Face the Nation*, Bob Schieffer asked this question: "Mr. Panetta, there's been a lot of antigovernment rhetoric, it comes over talk radio, it comes from various quarters. Do you think that that somehow has led these people to commit this act, do they feed on that kind of rhetoric, and what impact do you think it had?"

Carl Rowan, the late columnist, was quoted in a *Washington Post* story saying that, "Unless Gingrich and Dole and the Republicans say 'Am I inflaming a bunch of nuts?' you know we're going to have some more events. I am absolutely certain the harsher rhetoric of the Gingriches and the Doles . . . creates a climate of violence in America."

And David Broder had this to say in the *Washington Post*: "The bombing shows how dangerous it really is to inflame twisted minds with statements that suggest political opponents are enemies. For two years, Rush Limbaugh described this nation as 'America held hostage' to the policies of the liberal Democrats, as if the duly elected president and Congress were equivalent to the regime in Tehran. I think there will be less tolerance and fewer cheers for that kind of rhetoric."

The message was clear: Conservative talk radio and conservative politicians created an antigovernment atmosphere in America that spawned Timothy McVeigh and therefore were at least partially to blame for his terrorism. It's true, of course, that the atmosphere in which we live contributes to everything that happens in our culture. Calling people "kikes" or "niggers" makes it easier to see them as less than human and to treat them as something less than human. But to point fingers at talk radio for somehow encouraging Timothy McVeigh strikes me as a stretch at best; more likely it's just another opportunity for liberal journalists to blame conservatives for one more evil. And if this kind of connecting the dots is fair game, then should we also accuse

Americans who spoke out loudly and forcefully against the war in Vietnam—including many journalists—of contributing to the 1972 bombing of the Pentagon and to other sometimes deadly terrorism, perpetuated by fanatics on the Left? According to the media elites' rulebook, when liberals rant it's called free speech; when conservatives rant it's called incitement to terrorism.

As I watched the coverage of the attacks on the Pentagon and the World Trade Center, I wondered why I hadn't seen more stories on television news, long before these zealots flew their hijacked planes into American buildings, about the culture of anti-American hate that permeates so much of the Middle East—stories that might help explain how little Arab children can grow up to become fanatical suicide bombers.

If the media found it so important to discuss the malignant atmosphere created by "hot" conservative talk radio, then why didn't they find it important to delve into this malignant atmosphere that seems to have bred such maniacal killers? Why would journalists, so interested in connecting the dots when they thought they led to Rush Limbaugh, be so uninterested in connecting the dots when there might actually be dots to connect—*from hateful, widely held popular attitudes in much of the Arab world straight to the cockpits of those hijacked jetliners?*

One of the networks put an American Muslim woman on the news who said that no one blamed Christianity when McVeigh killed all those people. Why blame Islam now? The reporter interviewing this woman let her have her say, never bothering to point out that Timothy McVeigh didn't kill all those people in the name of Christianity. Suicide airplane hijackers, on the other hand, are people who actually believe their murderous acts will earn them a one-way ticket to Paradise.

Was what happened on September 11 a subversion of Islam, as pundits and journalists on network and cable TV told us over and over again? Or was it the result of an *honest* reading of the Koran? It's true, of course, that if taken too literally by uncritical minds, just about any

holy book can lead to bad things. Still, why are there no Christian suicide bombers, or Jewish suicide bombers, or Hindu suicide bombers,
or Buddhist suicide bombers, but no apparent shortage of Muslim suicide bombers? If Islam is "a religion of peace" as so many people from
President Bush on down were telling us (and, for what it's worth, I'm
prepared to believe that it is), then what exactly is it in the Koran that
so appeals to these Islamic fanatics? Don't look for that answer on the
network news. A Lexis-Nexis search going back to 1991 linking the
words "Koran" and "terrorist" produced absolutely nothing that told
us what the Koran actually says which *might* encourage a Muslim, no
matter how misguided, to commit acts of terrorism.

I understand that even to ask questions about a possible connection
between Islam and violence is to tread into politically incorrect terrain.
But it seems to me that the media need to go there anyway. And any network that can put thousands of stories on the air about sex and murder
should be able to give us a few on the atmosphere that breeds religious
zealotry. It might have helped us see what was coming on September 11.

In fact, I learned much more about the atmosphere that breeds suicide bombers from one short article in *Commentary* magazine than I
have from watching twenty years of network television news. In its
September 2001 issue (which came out before the attack on America),
there was an article by Fiamma Nirenstein, an Italian journalist based
in Israel, entitled "How Suicide Bombers Are Made." In it, she tells
about a "river of hatred" that runs through not just the most radical
of Arab nations but also much of what we like to think of as the "moderate" Arab world.

She tells us about a series of articles that ran in the leading government-
sponsored newspaper in Egypt, *Al Ahram*, about how Jews supposedly
use the blood of Christians to make matzah for Passover.

She tells us about a hit song in Cairo, Damascus, and the West Bank
with the catchy title "I Hate Israel."

Why didn't I know this? A computer check soon answered my question. On television, only CNN reported the "I Hate Israel" story. On radio, NPR did a piece. So did the *Christian Science Monitor* and the *Chicago Tribune*. The *Los Angeles Times* ran a short wire service story that said "'I Hate Israel'...made an overnight singing sensation of a working-class crooner."

Can you imagine if the big hit song in Israel was "I Hate Palestine" or "I Hate Arabs"? The *New York Times* would have put the story on page one and then run an editorial just to make sure we all got the message— that the song is indecent and contributes to an atmosphere of hate. And since the *Times* sets the agenda for the networks, Dan Rather, Tom Brokaw, and Peter Jennings would have all fallen into line and run big stories on their evening newscasts, too, saying the exact same thing. A week later, Mike Wallace would have landed in Tel Aviv looking absolutely mortified that those Jews would do such a thing.

And that's part of the problem. Despite the liberalism of the media, there is a subtle form of racism at work here. As Fiamma Nirenstein writes, "The Arabs, it is implicitly suggested, are a backward people, not to be held to civilized standards of the West." Of the Israelis, however, the American media expect much more. That is why a song called "I Hate Israel" becomes a big hit, and yet is not a news story. And it is why a series of stories in a government-sponsored newspaper—in a supposedly moderate country—about Jews killing Christians for their blood holds almost no interest for American journalists.

It's true that not long after the twin towers of the World Trade Center came tumbling down, the networks showed us pictures of Palestinians in East Jerusalem honking their horns, firing their guns into the air, and generally having a good old time celebrating the death of so many Americans in New York and Washington. They cheered "God is great" while they handed out candy, which is a tradition in the Arab world when something good happens.

It's not that there's been a total news blackout of anti-American hate in the Middle East—*Nightline* has done some good, intelligent work in this area—it's just that we need more than pictures of happy Palestinians reveling in the death of thousands of Americans. And we need more than what has become a staple of Middle East television news coverage: young children throwing stones at Israeli soldiers—the perfect made-for-television David and Goliath story. What we need are stories that connect the dots, not just back to Afghanistan and its backward and repressive Taliban government, but also between the fanatics in New York and Washington and a cultural environment in the Arab world where even "moderates" hand out candy to celebrate the massacre of Americans.

But here the media—apparently feeling squeamish about stories that put the "underdogs" in a bad light—keep us virtually in the dark. And it's not just little tidbits like "I Hate Israel" and articles about Jews taking Christian blood that I—and almost all Americans—knew nothing about. Here's a quick rundown of what goes on in much of the Middle East as reported by Ms. Nirenstein in *Commentary*—news that is virtually ignored on the big American TV networks:

> In Egypt and Jordan, news sources have repeatedly warned that Israel has distributed drug-laced chewing gum and candy, intended (it is said) to kill children and make women sexually corrupt....
>
> [Palestinian television] recently asserted that, far from being extermination camps, Chelmo, Dachau, and Auschwitz were in fact mere "places of disinfection."
>
> On April 13—observed in Israel as Holocaust Remembrance Day—the official Palestinian newspaper *Al-Hayat al-Jadida* featured a column... entitled "The Fable of the Holocaust."
>
> A columnist in Egypt's government-sponsored *Al-Akhbar* thus expressed his "thanks to Hitler, of blessed memory, who on

behalf of the Palestinians took revenge in advance on the most vile criminals on the face of the earth. Still, we do have a complaint against [Hitler], for his revenge on them was not enough."

In addition to these examples, Ms. Nirenstein cites a textbook for Syrian tenth graders which teaches them that "the logic of justice obligates the application of the single verdict [on the Jews] from which there is no escape: namely, that their criminal intentions be turned against them and that they be exterminated." And she notes that in June 2001, two weeks after the fatal collapse of a Jewish wedding hall in Jerusalem, Palestinian television broadcast a sermon by a Muslim imam praying that "this oppressive Knesset [Israel's parliament] will [similarly] collapse over the heads of the Jews."

I did not know any of that because it's simply not the kind of news that we normally get from the Middle East—certainly not from network evening newscasts or from *Dateline*, *20/20*, or *48 Hours*, three news magazine programs that are usually too busy peddling the trivial and sensational to bother with more significant stories. And besides, that kind of news makes liberal journalists uneasy. After all, these are the same people who bend over backwards to find "moral equivalence" between Palestinian terrorists who blow up discos in Tel Aviv filled with teenagers, on the one hand, and Israeli commandos who *preemptively* kill terrorist ringleaders *before* they send their suicide bombers into Israel on a mission to kill Jews, on the other.

On September 11, right after the networks showed us the pictures of Palestinians celebrating American deaths, they also showed us Yasser Arafat expressing his condolences and giving blood for the American victims. This, in its way, represented a kind of moral equivalence: while some Palestinians celebrate, the news anchors were suggesting, their leader does not; he is somber and, we're led to believe, absolutely shocked. But we could have done with a little less moral equivalence on the part of the press and a little more tough journalism. Someone should have asked the leader of the Palestinian people if he understood that the cultures that he and other "moderate" Arab leaders preside over "carefully nurture and inculcate resentments and hatreds against America and the non-Arab world," as a *Wall Street Journal* editorial put it. And if that's asking too much of a field reporter covering a seemingly shaken and distraught Arafat in the wake of September 11, then an anchor back in New York should have wondered out loud about that very connection.

But to have asked such a question might have been viewed as anti-Arab (and therefore pro-Israeli), and reporters and anchors would rather be stoned by an angry mob in Ramallah than be seen in that light. So we didn't learn that day if Chairman Arafat quite understood his role in the celebration he so deplored. Nor did we get an explanation on the news about why there were not thousands of other Arabs in the streets—on the West Bank or in Jerusalem or in the "moderate" Arab countries—expressing their *condolences*. Was it because they are afraid to show support for American victims of terrorism? Or was it because they, like the Palestinians we saw with great big smiles, didn't feel that bad about what happened?

If the networks can give us months and months of Chandra and JonBenet and Lorena Bobbitt and Joey Buttafuoco, then they can give us more than they do about the river of hatred that breeds suicide bombers.

But this is where journalists—given their liberal tendency to empathize with, and sometimes even root for, the "underdog"—run into a big problem: if they start to connect those ideological and religious dots, they may not like what they find.

American journalists who covered the civil rights struggle recognized the pathology of racism and rightly made no allowance for it. They understood that in order for evil to flourish in places throughout the

South, all it took was a few fundamentally bad people—while everybody else sat around making believe it wasn't happening, either because they were afraid or because they just didn't want to get involved.

The Middle East, of course, is a place with a long and troubled history. But it should be obvious that a place that turns "I Hate Israel" into a hit, that runs stories in its most important newspaper about Jews killing Christians for their blood, that faults Hitler *only because he did not kill more Jews,* and that celebrates the murder of thousands of innocent Americans is a place populated by many nasty people. Perhaps it has many good people, too, who just don't want to get involved. The point is, a story about all of this is at least as important as a story about Anne Heche and her sex life, even if sex does better in the ratings than disturbing news about raw, ignorant hatred in the world of Islam.

None of this is an argument that the media are intentionally pro-Arab. Rather, like the U.S. State Department, they are pro "moral equivalence." If they connect the dots with stories on the news about hit songs called "I Hate Israel" and all the rest, the Arab world will accuse the "Jewish-controlled" American media of being sympathetic to "Israeli oppression." If journalists—who were so willing to connect the dots when there was a belief that they led to Rush Limbaugh—connected *these* dots, they might find that there are a lot fewer moderates in those moderate places than they keep telling us about.

So they look the other way, which, as Ms. Nirenstein tells us, is not that easy. One has to turn "a determinedly blind eye to this river of hatred... [and] to be persuaded that, after all, 'everybody' in the Middle East really wants the same thing."

Obviously, there are legitimate issues about which there are differing viewpoints in the Middle East: Should Israel blow up the houses that belong to the families of terrorists? Should Israel allow the construction of new settlements on the West Bank? These are two that come quickly to mind.

But moral equivalence and the quest for evenhanded journalism should not stop the media from telling us more—much more in my view—about the kind of backwardness and hatred that is alive and well, *not just in places like Kabul and Baghdad*, but in "moderate" cities and villages all over the Arab world. Even if it means going against their liberal sensibilities and reporting that sometimes even the underdog can be evil.

Newzak 15

I **know it sounds crazy,** but I think Dan is caught in a time warp, living in a land where Richard Nixon is still president.

And still out to destroy him.

Watergate, Vietnam, lying, obstructing justice, hush money. Nixon was up to his eyeballs in trouble, and Rather was all over him. It's true that he wasn't Woodward or Bernstein—broadcast people almost never are—but Dan Rather was the toughest television guy on the beat, and every night on the *CBS Evening News*, Walter Cronkite would introduce a Rather piece, and Dan would hammer Nixon.

Whether it was the trademark Nixon paranoia or merely his charming vengefulness, the president and his palace guard despised Rather and called CBS brass more than a few times to see if they could get him transferred from the White House to someplace like Outer Mongolia. CBS wouldn't buckle, and Rather—the blue-collar kid whose daddy dug ditches—wasn't about to go weak in the knees and fold. He just got tougher.

But along the way I think he also became cynical and suspicious of *any* criticism. "Dan Rather can't distinguish between mainstream, legitimate criticism and criticism coming from extremists. It's all the same to him," is what Heyward told me after my op-ed came out.

And after the dark days of Richard Nixon, when Dan was constantly under siege, I believe he started seeing even well-meaning critics as enemies. Anyone who said there was a liberal bias on our news broadcasts was an extremist, practically by definition, as far as Dan was concerned. Every critic was a Richard Nixon lining Dan up in his sights. I think a little of Nixon's paranoia rubbed off on Dan.

In my own dark days after the op-ed, while I was waiting to find out if I had a job or not, I had a conversation with Jon Klein, the number two in command at CBS News, about why Dan—a guy who could be so kind and so funny and so generous—could also be so unforgiving. Rather had been telling people he would "never" forgive me. *Never!* And while I understood he wasn't going to throw a party to thank me for writing the op-ed, "never" seemed a bit extreme.

I mean, Rather has embraced people a lot worse than me. He practically kissed Fidel Castro in front of the whole evening news staff when the dictator showed up at CBS News studios on West 57th Street in the fall of 1995. Castro was in New York for the fiftieth anniversary of the signing of the United Nations Charter, and since CBS News was trying to get into Cuba to do a documentary, the brass invited Fidel over to show him that they were good guys who could be trusted. Never mind, for a moment, the irony that American journalists felt they had to prove to a communist dictator that *they* could be trusted. This was business.

So there they were, the two media grandees, Dan and Fidel, touring the studio where Dan does the evening news each night, smiling, laughing, bantering, looking like old pals who hadn't seen each other in years. Dan even gave Fidel a nice little gift—a baseball bat, because Fidel, as everyone knows, loves baseball. In the old days, he actually was offered a contract to play for the New York Giants, which he turned down, in the words of one reporter, "to become a communist free agent instead."

But when you think about it, all the smiles and all the laughs—business or no business—makes a lot of sense. After all, to a lot of liberals, Fidel isn't a communist dictator. I mean, *technically* he is. They know, for example, that he hasn't allowed a free election in the last forty years or so, that he doesn't tolerate dissent, and that he'd rather drink battery acid on the rocks with a touch of lime than allow a free press. Mere technicalities. The way they see it, to describe Fidel Castro simply as a dictator is so . . . *uncool* comes to mind. To the *cognoscenti*—especially the liberal *cognoscenti* in the media—Fidel is a *celebrity*. So what if he doesn't tolerate freedom of the press? That doesn't mean an American newsman can't like the guy, does it?

Castro—who locks people up if they look at him funny—The Dan embraces. Me—I write a little op-ed piece calling the media elites a bunch of lefties, and—he'll "never" forgive.

Go figure.

Jon Klein, like Rather, thought I had crossed the line with my op-ed, and in terms of etiquette Jon and everybody else were absolutely right. Miss Manners would never approve of what I had done. But Klein wasn't apoplectic over it the way Rather and a lot of the others were. So I asked him what it was about Rather that could make him so implacable when he thought you crossed him.

"You have to understand that Dan Rather is Richard Nixon," Jon told me. "If he sees you as an enemy *even for a second*, you're an enemy for life. And like Nixon, Rather must destroy his enemies."

The irony didn't escape Klein. This time it was Rather—just like his nemesis Richard Nixon two decades before—who was confusing dissent with betrayal, even treason.

"Now Rather has become what he detested," Jon told me.

After the op-ed came out, cracks didn't appear in the earth, airplanes didn't drop out of the sky, people didn't riot in the streets, the stock market didn't crash, and the sun kept coming up in the east.

This was all working in my favor.

Then out of the blue, I got a boost from none other than Michael Jordan. Too bad it wasn't the basketball player Michael Jordan. That would have gotten me out of the doghouse once and for all. The Michael Jordan who took my side, unfortunately, was only the chairman of Westinghouse, the company that owned CBS at the time. Technically speaking he was Dan's and everyone else's boss—but in the halls of CBS News, Michael Jordan wasn't such a big deal.

Jordan did an interview in *USAir Magazine*, of all places, and said, "I think his [Goldberg's] criticism is fair. I think all the networks can do a better job at providing a more objective and balanced perspective. Goldberg's account was inspired not so much by the content as by the patronizing tone of the coverage. That's very typical when somebody criticizes something like the flat tax. I think it's wrong, because a high percentage of the American public has been lectured to since the early sixties and is a little fed up with it."

The Michael Jordan interview had little to do with it, but soon afterward, the powers that be at CBS News decided to take me back. Indeed, about two months after I wrote that "the old argument that the networks and other 'media elites' have a liberal bias is so blatantly true that it's hardly worth discussing anymore," I was back on the job.

But my agent at the time, Richard Leibner, whose biggest client is Dan Rather, warned me that it's never the same after such turmoil, that the bad blood lingers for a very long time.

He was right.

Before the blowup I had started doing opinion pieces for Dan's evening newscast. "Analysis" is what they technically called it because the word "commentary" made them nervous. This was going to be a very prestigious assignment, mainly since only Eric Sevareid and Bill Moyers had done analysis on the evening news before me.

But when Heyward took me back he said no more commentary because "you might be seen as a conservative balance to an otherwise liberal broadcast . . . and since the evening news isn't a liberal broadcast, we can't let you do analysis anymore."

There is a technical word to describe this kind of reasoning. The word is "horseshit."

So, I did some straight reporting for the evening news, but mainly I bounced around on prime-time magazine programs, the names of which will be answers in trivia contests. Who will ever forget *Coast to Coast*?

Everybody!

And when the last show I was on fell in the summer of 1998, *Public Eye with Bryant Gumbel*, I didn't know what was in store for me.

My contract was coming up for renewal, and this would be the perfect time for CBS News to let me go, quietly, without the noise it would have caused if they flat-out fired me right after the op-ed was published.

But there was a new magazine CBS News had just decided to do—a second *60 Minutes*, *60 Minutes II*, and even Andrew Heyward, the president of CBS News, said "it was a no-brainer" that I should be one of the correspondents. Except for one thing. Andrew said he wouldn't interfere with the decision of the show's new executive producer, Jeff Fager—the same Jeff Fager who ran the *CBS Evening News* when my op-ed appeared and who had been one of its many critics.

I met with Fager in his office on West 57th Street in New York on August 11, 1998, at Andrew's urging. A meeting couldn't hurt, Andrew figured. We talked about the new show for a while, but I sensed a tension during the conversation, so I asked if there was a problem.

Yeah, he said—the *Wall Street Journal* piece.

"I'll never be able to put that behind me," he said.

"Never?" I said to him.

This was the same word Rather was using, saying he would "never" forgive me for what I had done. It was no secret that when Dan Rather sneezes, Jeff Fager (and every other executive producer who works for Dan) catches cold. And since Dan was the lead correspondent on the new *60 Minutes II*, and since Fager was using the very same language Dan was using, I knew I was a dead man walking.

"But I won't let that [the op-ed] influence my decision," he said, as our meeting was ending.

I was about to say, *"Then why the fuck did you just bring it up,"* but I knew that wouldn't help my chances of getting on the show. Still, I knew, as Texas Dan might have phrased it, that my chances were someplace between slim and none—and slim just left town.

Fager said he would keep me in mind for one of the correspondent slots, which we both knew wasn't true. A month later, on September 15, 1998, he made it official. Fager called me at home in Miami and said I would not be on the show. It's true: payback is a bitch.

That's when I decided that I would no longer let any of them continue to punish me. Day in and day out, they would scrutinize politicians and business people and doctors and lawyers and put what they found on television for millions to see. But they would "never" let me off the hook for scrutinizing them.

What a bunch of hypocrites, I kept thinking, these people who examine anybody and everybody's life but will "never" forgive me for writing about their liberal bias.

The Dan Rathers of the world don't try to crush you if they think you're full of crap. They simply ignore you. It's when you taunt them with the truth that they get really frantic and try to inflict pain, if for no other reason than to show everybody else in the newsroom that the cost of breaking the sacred code of *omerta* will be very high.

Reinhold Niebuhr, the American theologian, might as well have been talking about thin-skinned evening news stars when he said,

"Frantic orthodoxy is never rooted in faith but in doubt." Dan's frantic orthodoxy, his supposed certainty that anyone who accuses the media elites of having a liberal bias must be a right-wing political activist, is rooted not in his faith that he's right, but in his doubt that maybe, just maybe, the critics are on to something.

I didn't want to work at CBS News anymore. And it was pretty clear they didn't want me. I asked for a meeting with Heyward, and two days after Fager told me I wouldn't be on *60 Minutes II*, I met with Andrew in his office in New York and told him I would leave CBS News and never show my face again if he would let me stay until May 31, 2000, when my pension would kick in.

He agreed to let me stay on, accepting my resignation and making no effort to keep me at CBS News. So in the summer of 2000, I left after twenty-eight years.

On July 4, 2001, there was a ray of sunshine. Peter Jennings told the *Boston Globe*, "Those of us who went into journalism in the '50s or '60s, it was sort of a liberal thing to do. Save the world." Obvious, yes, but it's important that Jennings actually said it. Publicly.

But even more important is what he said regarding the question of fairness and balance. "Conservative voices in the U.S.," Peter acknowledged, "have not been as present as they might have been and should have been in the media."

Given that this came out on the Fourth of July, maybe it would be the beginning of a revolution. Maybe Dan and Tom and their reporters and producers would be next, admitting what millions of their viewers, past and present, have long known. And maybe they would use Peter's observation as an opportunity to think more deeply about their biases and, after all these years, start to make things right.

But I'm not optimistic. The pattern by now is too ingrained: some-one makes the liberal bias charge, the target of the accusation—Dan or

Tom or some lesser star—denies it and accuses the accuser of having an agenda, or as in Peter's case—the most civil of the bunch—says that "bias is very largely in the eye of the beholder"—even while he's admitting that the bias is very largely in the hands of the networks.

It has become too visceral. Dan, the one I know the best, can't think seriously about the criticism since he's too busy taking it personally, as an attack on his integrity, which it sometimes is but often is not.

So how much has really changed? They continue to slant the news and then—Peter's media culpa notwithstanding—deny they're doing it. They are not lying. They just don't understand, which is precisely why they need to listen more carefully to the critics, especially the ones who come to them without political and ideological baggage.

Now that I'm not part of the organization, I watch Dan only occasionally on the evening news, and I just smile. Why does he feel the need, I wonder, to tell his audience about President Bush's "Republican-right agenda"? The man was in office less than a week and already Dan has spotted a "Republican-right agenda." Why, I wonder, did he never talk about President Clinton and his "Democratic-left agenda"?

Why does Bob Schieffer tell us that John Ashcroft has "conservative views" but that the organizations that opposed him during confirmation hearings were simply a collection of "rights groups"? Why is it so hard for Bob to put the word "liberal" in front of "rights groups"?

I watch the news, and Dan is mouthing words about Congress or the president's tax plan—but it's just Newzak, the TV news version of elevator music. On the TV, Dan is telling us about how President Bush is "keeping up his drumbeat of negative talk about the health of the U.S. economy and using that in his efforts to sell Congress on a big tax cut."

The Newzak goes on and on.

All I can do is what millions of Americans have been doing for years. I take one last look at my good friend Dan, blow him a good-bye kiss, aim my remote right at his eyeball . . . and click the button marked "off."

Appendix A
The Editorials

Networks Need a Reality Check
By Bernard Goldberg
February 13, 1996
Wall Street Journal

There are **lots of reasons** fewer people are watching network news, and one of them, I'm more convinced than ever, is that our viewers simply don't trust us. And for good reason.

The old argument that the networks and other "media elites" have a liberal bias is so blatantly true that it's hardly worth discussing any-more. No, we don't sit around in dark corners and plan strategies on how we're going to slant the news. We don't have to. It comes naturally to most reporters.

Which brings us to a recent "Reality Check" on the *CBS Evening News*, reported by Eric Engberg, a longtime friend. His subject was Steve Forbes's flat tax. It's not just Democrats and some Republican presidential candidates who don't like the flat tax—it's also a lot of big-time reporters. The flat tax rubs them the wrong way. Which is fair enough—until their bias makes its way into their reporting. And Mr. Engberg's report set new standards for bias.

He starts out saying: "Steve Forbes pitches his flat-tax scheme as an economic elixir, good for everything that ails us." Sure, the words "scheme" and "elixir" are loaded, conjuring up images of Doctor Feelgood selling worthless junk out of the back of his wagon. But this is nothing more than a prelude—warm-up material to get us into the right frame of mind.

The report shows Mr. Forbes saying the U.S. economy can grow twice as fast if we remove "obstacles, starting with the tax code." Mr. Forbes may be right or wrong about this, so Mr. Engberg lets us know which it is. "Time out" he shouts in his signature style. "Economists say nothing like that has ever actually happened."

He then introduces us to William Gale of the Brookings Institution, who says "It doesn't seem plausible to think that we're going to have a whole new economy or economic Renaissance Age due to tax reform."

CBS News instructs its reporters and producers to identify people in a way that will help the audience understand any political bias they might have. We are told, for example, to identify the Heritage Foundation as "a conservative think tank." I have done this on more than one occasion, myself. It's a good policy.

But where was the identification of the Brookings Institution as "a liberal think tank"? Might that influence Mr. Gale's take on the flat tax? Instead, Mr. Gale was presented to America simply as an expert with no tax ax to grind.

Mr. Engberg then shows Mr. Forbes saying: "A flat tax would enable this economy to grow. That would mean more revenues for Washington." To this, Mr. Engberg tells the audience: "That was called supply-side economics under President Reagan: Less taxes equal more revenue. It didn't work out that way." Immediately after this we hear Mr. Engberg ask this question of Mr. Gale: "Is it fair to say the last time we tried something like this, we ended up with these hideous deficits?" To which Gale obediently replies, "It's perfectly fair to say that."

Mr. Engberg continues: "And if we try it again, your fear is . . . ?" And Mr. Gale replies: ". . . that we end up with the same problem again."

But haven't other experts argued that we wound up with "hideous deficits" not because of the tax cut but because of increased spending? And to the best of my knowledge, neither Mr. Forbes nor any other flat-tax proponent is suggesting we increase spending.

(Part of the problem is that most reporters and editors—television and print—are total dunces when it comes to the economy. Most don't know a capital gain from a mutual fund. This, as much as bias, in some cases leads to the kind of reporting we see on the flat tax and a lot of other economic issues.)

One thing to remember about network news is that it steals just about everything from print. So if the *New York Times* is against the flat tax, and the *Washington Post* is against the flat tax, the networks can't, and won't, be far behind.

Mr. Engberg concludes his piece à la David Letterman by saying that "Forbes's Number One Wackiest Flat-Tax Promise" is the candidate's belief that it would give parents "more time to spend with their children and each other."

Can you imagine, in your wildest dreams, a network news reporter calling Hillary Clinton's health care plan "wacky"? Can you imagine any editor allowing it?

Finally, Mr. Engberg says: "The fact remains: the flat tax is a giant, untested theory. One economist suggested, before we put it in, we should test it out someplace—like Albania."

"Reality Check" suggests the viewers are going to get the facts. And then they can make up their mind. As Mr. Engberg might put it: "Time out!" You'd have a better chance of getting the facts someplace else—like Albania.

Blowing the Whistle on CBS News
February 15, 1996
New York Post editorial page

CBS News, which prides itself on its bold willingness to expose the dark secrets of corporate America, has apparently discovered that the truth hurts.

In Tuesday's *Wall Street Journal*, veteran CBS correspondent Bernard Goldberg wrote a column on the political bias that informs network news. Even though Goldberg said nothing even mildly controversial, his article has already ignited a firestorm at Black Rock.

And what does Goldberg write that so outrages his colleagues and superiors at CBS News?

He notes, for starters, that "the old argument that the networks...have a liberal bias is so blatantly true that it's hardly worth discussing anymore." Again, this amounts to rehearsing the obvious; it would be of little or no interest were it not for the fact of Goldberg's standing as a network news employee.

He goes on to dissect the political slant of a *CBS Evening News* segment—broadcast by reporter Eric Engberg—on GOP candidate Steve Forbes's flat-tax proposal. After noting that Engberg employed loaded language to influence the viewer's perception Engberg's discussion of the tax plan included tendentious terms like "scheme" and "elixir"—Goldberg points out that Engberg allowed an analyst from the Brookings Institution to disparage the Forbes proposal without pausing to acknowledge Brookings's decidedly liberal orientation.

This, apparently, represents a departure from standard practice at CBS—reporters are meant to identify the political orientation of the analysts who appear or the institutions they represent. As Goldberg notes, it's hard to imagine a Forbes enthusiast from, say, the Heritage Foundation showing up on a newscast absent a comment to the effect that Heritage is a "conservative" think tank.

Engberg, it seems, ended his piece by calling the flat tax "wacky." This prompts Goldberg to ask an uncomplicated question: "Can you imagine, in your wildest dreams, a network news reporter calling Hillary Clinton's health plan 'wacky'?"

Of course not.

Engberg's segment—and this is Goldberg's larger message—bespeaks a wider syndrome. Night after night, the networks present the news with a leftish tinge—sometimes to discredit the California Civil Rights Initiative (an anti-racial-quotas ballot measure); sometimes to misrepresent the GOP's Medicare reform plan. And most reporters don't even realize that their work is informed by ideological bias.

CBS is working itself into a state of high dudgeon over Goldberg's decision to go public with his views. *Evening News* anchor Dan Rather "deplores" the whole situation. CBS News president Andrew Heyward is said to be livid. No one, however, appears ready to dispute the details in which Goldberg's analysis is grounded.

We can sympathize with the suggestion that trust within a company is undermined when isolated individuals bare dirty linen in public. But it comes with little grace for CBS News to take refuge in this line of argument. After all, many Americans were introduced to the concept of corporate "whistle-blowers" by CBS journalists.

Only recently, *60 Minutes* devoted an entire program to a former tobacco executive—"Deep Cough"—who chronicled the alleged misdeeds of his ex-employer. The show, in fact, made a point of acknowledging "Deep Cough's" courage and tenacity. At least Bernard Goldberg had the courage to identify himself by name.

Meanwhile, it's worth remembering that whistle-blowers can tell all kinds of truths. And it is just as important for the American people to understand how bias taints the news disseminated by the major networks as it is for them to grasp the alleged inner workings of tobacco companies.

Here's to Bernard Goldberg, whose insights are especially valuable because they come from someone with intimate knowledge of the way the television news process works.

On Media Bias, Network Stars Are Rather Clueless
By Bernard Goldberg
May 24, 2001
Wall Street Journal

Dan Rather has been on television more than usual lately, popping up all over the place promoting his book about American success stories and along the way wearily denying that he's the left-wing devil some conservatives think he is.

It's the same old story as far as Dan is concerned. The right thinks he's an unapologetic liberal who slants the news leftward—not because he is, but because his critics are so hopelessly biased themselves that they wouldn't know straight news when they saw it. As another evening star, Peter Jennings, told Larry King recently, bias often is in the eye of the beholder. And since Tom Brokaw also has publicly denied a liberal bias, it's official. There is none. It's all a figment of the reactionary imagination. Case closed.

Except, as just about everyone who lives between Manhattan and Malibu knows, there is a leftward tilt on the big-three evening newscasts. A poll last year by *Brill's Content* showed that 74 percent of Republicans

Nixon could have beaten George McGovern in 1972: "Nobody I know voted for Nixon." Never mind that Nixon carried forty-nine states. She wasn't kidding.

If there is one group that is uniquely unqualified to comment on liberal bias, it's the big-time media stars. So Dan and Tom and Peter: Stop telling us that we're the problem and start thinking about what liberal bias really means.

Appendix B
The Response

My original *Wall Street Journal* editorial on media bias provoked a flood of sympathetic mail. Some of it came from friends in the news profession (such as my CBS colleague Andy Rooney) with whom the sentiments I expressed struck a chord; most came from a viewership exasperated with increasingly blatant bias on the part of the networks. Here are but a few samples.

13 Feb 1996

Bernie:

In the future, if you have any derogatory
remarks to make about CBS News or one of your
co-workers....I hope you'll do the same thing again.

Regards,

[signature]

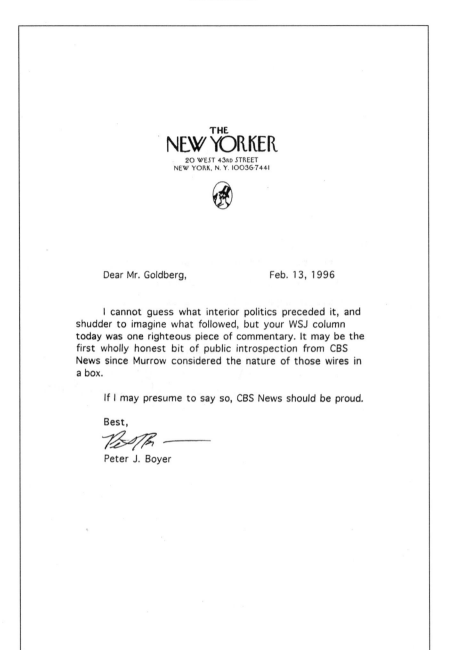

THE

NEW YORKER

20 WEST 43RD STREET
NEW YORK, N. Y. 10036-7441

Dear Mr. Goldberg,   Feb. 13, 1996

I cannot guess what interior politics preceded it, and shudder to imagine what followed, but your WSJ column today was one righteous piece of commentary. It may be the first wholly honest bit of public introspection from CBS News since Murrow considered the nature of those wires in a box.

If I may presume to say so, CBS News should be proud.

Best,

Peter J. Boyer

THE RESPONSE

03/13/96 08:59 ▓▓▓▓▓▓▓▓▓▓▓▓

BERNARD GOLDBERG

FROM: ▓▓▓▓▓ NEWS DIR. ▓▓▓▓▓▓▓▓▓▓

DATE: 3/12/96

I'M SORRY TO READ IN USA TODAY ABOUT YOUR DIFFICULTIES. I HOPE THEY AREN'T AS BAD AS THE ARTICLE SUGGESTS..BUT I FEAR THEY ARE.

NEVERTHELESS, THANKS FOR HAVING THE BALLS TO WRITE THE COLUMN. IT NEEDED SAYING AND YOU DID A GOOD JOB ON THE PIECE.

I CAN'T FIGURE PEOPLE WHO CLAIM TO LOVE JOURNALISM BUT WHEN SOMEONE COMES ALONG AND POINTS OUT SOMETHING THAT NEEDS ATTENTION, THEY CAN'T HANDLE IT.

DON'T LOSE ANY STOMACH LINING OVER THIS.

EXCELSIOR,

Bob

APPENDIX B

H. Alan Keener

February 14, 1996

Mr. Bernard Goldberg
CBS News
524 West 57th Street
New York, New York 10019

Dear Mr. Goldberg:

Bravo on "Networks Need a Reality Check." You've said what many have thought for a long time. Coming from someone within broadcast news, your statement is doubly authentic. As you so eloquently point out, the issue is not bias per se - most people, journalists included, have biases - but how that bias is revealed by journalists. All too often, the liberal media tend to load the dice in favor of their viewpoint, deriding as kooky or somewhat unworthy of serious discussion those positions they disagree with. That is why serious students of broadcast news tend to watch the Lehrer News Hour, where a serious attempt is made to present all sides of an issue.

It is to be hoped that some of your network colleagues will take your criticism to heart. In the meantime, I hope you don't lose your job!

Sincerely yours,

H. Alan Keener

HERBERT K. RUSSELL

███████

███████ ──

██████

February 17, 1996

Bernard Goldberg,

I thought all the heroes were dead--until I read your article in
the Wall Street Journal for February 13, 1996, re liberal bias in
the media. Please accept my congratulations and thanks for a
job well done.

Liberal bias among the television networks has done something
that market forces could not have engendered, the revitalization of
radio. Rush Limbaugh would never have become the success he has if
the firm of Rather, Brokaw, and Jennings had done its job. Instead,
they failed, as you so ably point out.

But all is not lost for television news outlets. There is a market
ready and waiting for any network that chooses to deliver a truthful
and unbiased account of the day's events as the evening news. It
will be interesting to see whether any of the networks follow this
line of reasoning, or whether they will finish burying themselves
in the holes they are digging.

Best wishes,

Herbert K Russell

Herbert K. Russell

cc: President, CBS News

Richard C. Asper

█████████████████

Bernard Goldberg
c/o CBS-News
524 West 57th St.
New York, NY 10019-2902

Dear Mr. Goldberg,

     Where are you? Since you wrote that op-ed piece for the *Wall Street Journal* exposing the media's liberal bias, it's like you disappeared. Never fear, I have an idea! Please paste your photo to the milk carton below, and we will fax it out to all the major news organizations in the country.

Your
picture
here

CBS
Milk
2% Fact

Have you seen this man?
<u>Name</u>: Bernard Goldberg
Subject has been missing
since he told the truth about
the media's liberal bias.
We fear the worst.

Sincerely,
R. Asper

6/5/96